# Oliver Twist

Charles **Dickens**

Illustrated by **Fabio Visintin**
Retold by **Gina D. B. Clemen**

Series Editor: Robert Hill
Editor: Sara Servente
Design and art direction: Nadia Maestri
Computer graphics: Carlo Cibrario-Sent, Simona Corniola
Picture research: Alice Graziotin

© 2013 Black Cat

First edition: January 2013

DEALINK, DEAFLIX are trademarks licensed by De Agostini SpA

Picture credits:
Istockphoto; Dreams Time; Shutterstock Images; Getty Images: 4; Tips Images: 40; © Bettmann/CORBIS: 41, 90; Lewis W. Hine/Getty Images: 91; © MEDUSA/WebPhoto: 92, 93.

All rights reserved. No part of this book may be reproduced, stored in a retrieval system, or transmitted, in any form or by any means, electronic, mechanical, photocopying, recording or otherwise, without the written permission of the publisher.

We would be happy to receive your comments and suggestions, and give you any other information concerning our material.
info@blackcat-cideb.com
blackcat-cideb.com

The design, production and distribution of educational materials for the Black Cat brand are managed in compliance with the rules of Quality Management System which fulfils the requirements of the standard ISO 9001 (Rina Cert. No. 24298/02/S - IQNet Reg. No. IT-80096)

Printed in Italy by Italgrafica, Novara

# Contents

**CHARLES DICKENS** — 4

| | | |
|---|---|---|
| CHAPTER **ONE** | Young Oliver | 9 |
| CHAPTER **TWO** | Mr Sowerberry's Shop | 17 |
| CHAPTER **THREE** | Oliver Walks to London | 25 |
| CHAPTER **FOUR** | Fagin's Strange Game | 33 |
| CHAPTER **FIVE** | Mr Brownlow | 43 |
| CHAPTER **SIX** | A Terrible Night | 51 |
| CHAPTER **SEVEN** | Oliver's New Home | 59 |
| CHAPTER **EIGHT** | Nancy's Secret | 67 |
| CHAPTER **NINE** | London Bridge | 76 |
| CHAPTER **TEN** | Monks, Sikes and the Others | 82 |

| | | |
|---|---|---|
| **DOSSIERS** | Crime in Victorian London | 40 |
| | Child Labour | 90 |

**FILMOGRAPHY** — 92

**UNDERSTANDING THE TEXT** — 13, 22, 30, 37, 42, 48, 56, 64, 73, 80, 88

**PET** PET-style activities — 8, 15, 16, 22, 23, 24, 30, 31, 32, 38, 39, 42, 48, 50, 56, 64, 65, 66, 75, 80, 81, 88, 89, 94

**T: GRADE 4** Trinity-style activities (Grade 4) — 14, 37

**AFTER READING** — 94

The text is recorded in full.

 These symbols indicate the beginning and end of the passages linked to the listening activities.

Charles Dickens

# Charles Dickens

Charles Dickens, one of the world's greatest authors, was born in Portsmouth, England, on 7 February 1812. He was the second of eight children. He had a happy childhood and loved reading all kinds of books.

When Dickens was only twelve years old his father went to prison because he had serious money problems. Young Dickens had to leave school and went to work in a factory. He worked long hours in very bad conditions and he never forgot this terrible experience.

When Dickens was nineteen years old he became a newspaper reporter for *The Mirror of Parliament*. Soon he began writing short stories for magazines. In Dickens's times novels were usually published in parts in magazines: every week or month a part of the story appeared in the magazine. This went on for many months until the story was finished. A lot of people bought the magazines to read the story.

In April 1836 Dickens married Catherine Hogarth. They had ten children.

*The Pickwick Papers* was Dickens's first novel. It was published in monthly parts. He finished it in 1837 and it was a great success.

During his life Dickens met many people; they were young, old, rich, poor, happy, sad, kind and unkind. He wrote about them in his wonderful novels.

Dickens lived during the Victorian Age and his books often talk about poverty and the many social problems of the time. He wrote fourteen major novels: some of them are *Oliver Twist* (1837-38), *A Christmas Carol* (1843), *David Copperfield* (1849-50), *Nicholas Nickleby* (1854) and *Great Expectations* (1860-1).

Dickens travelled to Italy, Switzerland, France and the United States, where he read extracts from some of his novels to the public in New York and Boston. The Americans liked his books a lot.

He died at the age of 58 and was buried in Poets' Corner in Westminster Abbey in London.

## 1 COMPREHENSION CHECK

**Are the following questions true (T) or false (F)? Correct the false ones.**

A B

1 Charles Dickens was born in London, England in 1812.
2 Dickens's father worked in a prison.
3 Young Dickens did not like working in a factory.
4 Dickens worked for a newspaper when he was nineteen years old.
5 Dickens's first novel was not successful, but he continued to write books.
6 The Victorian Age had many social problems.
7 People in New York and Boston went to listen to Dickens.

# The Characters

*First row from left:* Fagin, Bill Sikes, Monks, Nancy, Mr Sowerberry, Rose Maylie, Mrs Bedwin
*Second row from left:* Oliver, Jack Dawkins "the Dodger", Mr Bumble, Noah Claypole, Mr Brownlow, Doctor Losberne

# BEFORE YOU READ

## 1 VOCABULARY
**Match the words with their meaning.**

1 ☐ workhouse  A warm breakfast food made from cereal and milk or water.
2 ☐ orphan  B a child who has no parents to look after him.
3 ☐ orphanage  C a place where very poor people live.
4 ☐ porridge  D to continue to live in difficult circumstances.
5 ☐ to survive  E a place where orphans live.

**PET**

## 2 LISTENING
**Listen to the first part of Chapter One and choose the correct answer — A, B or C.**

track 03

1 Oliver Twist's mother
 A ☐ lived in a workhouse.
 B ☐ died in a workhouse.
 C ☐ knew a doctor at the workhouse.

2 Oliver's mother didn't have
 A ☐ a wedding ring.
 B ☐ a coat.
 C ☐ a pair of gloves.

3 Until the age of nine Oliver lived in
 A ☐ a workhouse.
 B ☐ a church.
 C ☐ an orphanage.

4 The people in the workhouse ate
 A ☐ bread on Sundays.
 B ☐ an onion on Sundays.
 C ☐ porridge three times a week.

5 The people in the workhouse were always
 A ☐ sleepy.
 B ☐ thirsty.
 C ☐ hungry.

8

CHAPTER **ONE**

# Young Oliver

A long time ago every town in England had a workhouse. This was a house for very poor people and a very sad place to live. Oliver Twist was born in a workhouse. His mother, who was a young woman, was very ill when she came to the workhouse.

A doctor and an old woman were with her. After Oliver was born his mother said, 'I want to see my baby and then die.'

The old woman and the doctor looked at each other.

'You're too young to die,' said the old woman.

The doctor put the little baby in his mother's arms and she kissed the baby; then she died.

'Goodness!'[1] said the doctor, 'she's dead.'

'The poor dear!' said the old woman. 'She came here late last night.'

'Where's she from?' asked the doctor.

'No one knows where she's from,' replied the old woman.

1. **Goodness** : an expression of surprise.

# Oliver Twist

The doctor looked at the young woman's left hand and said, 'There's no wedding ring; she wasn't married. Good night.' He put on his hat, coat and gloves and left.

The old woman began to dress the baby with some old clothes. Little Oliver was alone in the world; he was an orphan and no one loved him.

When Oliver was small his home was an orphanage, where he lived with other young orphans. The children of the orphanage were given very little food and very little love. Many of the orphans died because they were cold and hungry. The orphanage was a unhappy place. Oliver survived, although he was pale, small and thin.

At the age of nine Oliver had to leave the orphanage and the only friends he had. This made him very sad because now he was really alone in the world. He was taken to a workhouse, a miserable place where he had to work long hours. He was given only one small bowl of porridge three times a day and an onion twice a week. Because Sunday was a special day he was given a small piece of bread.

Oliver and the other people at the workhouse were always cold, hungry and unhappy. They never asked for a second bowl of porridge because they were afraid. However, after three months of hunger and unhappiness Oliver and the others decided to do something. They discussed the matter and decided that Oliver had to ask the master for more porridge. So that evening he took his small empty bowl to the master of the workhouse, who was a big man with a white apron.

'Please, sir,' said Oliver looking at the master, 'I want some more.'

The master was very surprised and stared at him. Then he hit Oliver with his big wooden spoon.

'Mr Bumble,' cried the master. 'Please come here!'

Mr Bumble, who was an important officer in the town, rushed into the room and said, 'What's this nonsense?'

# Oliver Twist

'This young boy asked for *more porridge!*' exclaimed the master, whose face was red.

'What?' asked Mr Bumble. 'Did I hear you correctly? *More porridge?*'

'Yes sir, *more porridge?*' replied the master, holding up the big wooden spoon.

Mr Bumble took Oliver to the office of the directors of the workhouse and said, 'Oliver Twist asked for more porridge!'

'For more porridge?' they cried, looking at each other. 'This boy must leave the workhouse immediately!'

Mr Bumble put Oliver in a cold, dark room for one whole week. Every morning Mr Bumble opened the door of the dark room and hit Oliver with a stick in front of his friends. Poor Oliver did nothing but cry all day long and he couldn't sleep at night because he was terribly cold, hungry and sad.

One day Mr Bumble met his friend Mr Sowerberry, who was a tall, thin man. He made coffins [2] for dead bodies, and many of the dead bodies came from the workhouse.

'Do you need a boy to work in your shop?' asked Mr Bumble. 'We'll give you five pounds if you take him.'

'Hmm,' said Mr Sowerberry, 'yes, I need a boy and I need the five pounds. I'll take him!'

That evening Mr Bumble took Oliver to Mr Sowerberry's shop. When they got near the shop Oliver looked at Mr Bumble and started crying.

'Oh, sir, I want to be a good boy. I am a very little boy, sir. And it is so… lonely. So very lonely!' Oliver couldn't stop crying and his thin, pale face was covered with tears.

2. **coffin** :

# UNDERSTANDING THE TEXT

## 1 COMPREHENSION CHECK
Match the phrases 1-8 to the phrases A-L to make complete sentences about Chapter One. There are four phrases you do not need to use.

1. ☐ Oliver Twist's mother died
2. ☐ The old woman did not know
3. ☐ The orphanage was a very sad place
4. ☐ Oliver and the other people at the workhouse
5. ☐ No one at the workhouse asked for more porridge
6. ☐ Oliver had to leave the workhouse
7. ☐ Mr Sowerberry
8. ☐ Mr Bumble asked Mr Sowerberry

A  because the children were always hungry and no one loved them.
B  made coffins for dead bodies.
C  because they were afraid.
D  was the director of the workhouse.
E  immediately after Oliver was born.
F  if he needed a boy to work for him.
G  a month after Oliver was born.
H  were always hungry, cold and unhappy.
I  because he was very lonely.
J  where Oliver's mother came from.
K  because he asked for more porridge.
L  because he didn't like Mr Sowerberry.

## 2 VOCABULARY
**A  Circle the odd words out and explain why.**

1. porridge   meat   fish   poultry
2. bowl   cup   dish   box
3. doctor   teacher   parent   engineer
4. onion   orange   carrot   spinach
5. Turkey   England   Irish   Italy
6. hat   coat   gloves   ring

**B   Now complete the sentences with the odd words.**

A   Is Patrick an .............................. name?
B   They put all the books in a big .............................. .
C   Oliver was tired of eating .............................. every day.
D   He ate an .............................. at breakfast.
E   Oliver did not have a .............................. to look after him.
F   Oliver's mother did not have a wedding .............................. on her finger.

## 3  WRITING

Read the information about workhouses and fill in the gaps with the correct past tense of the verb in the box. The first is done for you.

> have to (x2)   know   work   mean   go   do
> wear   start   be (x2)   can   want

In Great Britain after 1834 poor people who had no job or home (0) ....went......... to live in a workhouse, where they (1) .................... work for their food. They (2) .................... hard and (3) .................... unpleasant jobs.

Women, children and men (4) .................... stay in different living and working areas and they (5) .................... not speak to one another. These people (6) .................... uniforms and this (7) .................... that everyone looked the same and everyone outside (8) .................... they were poor and lived in a workhouse. The day at the workhouse (9) .................... at six o'clock in the morning and everyone was in bed by eight o'clock at night.

There (10) .................... very little food and it didn't taste good. Only porridge, soup, potatoes, cheese, bread and little cooked meat (11) .................... on the menu. No one (12) .................... to live in such a terrible place!

T : GRADE 4

## 4  SPEAKING - FOOD

Oliver never had enough good food at the workhouse. Talk to your partner about your favourite food and use these questions to help you.

1   What's your favourite food and why?
2   Do you know how to make it?
3   Who does the cooking at your house?
4   What's your favourite restaurant or fast-food place?

### 5 NOTICES

Look at the text in each question and choose the correct answer — A, B or C.

1. **Dogs not allowed inside inn from noon to 2.00 pm**
   - A ☐ Dogs must never enter the inn.
   - B ☐ Dogs can enter the inn between noon and 2 pm.
   - C ☐ Dogs can enter the inn before noon and after 2 pm.

2. **LONDON BANK**
   Open 9.30 – 4.30 pm
   We close at 3 pm on Fridays.
   Except Saturdays and Sundays
   - A ☐ The bank is open five days a week.
   - B ☐ You can't go to the bank on Monday at noon.
   - C ☐ The bank is closed on Friday.

3. **DANGER! Road in bad conditions. Ice on the road. Keep on the left.**
   - A ☐ You must not walk on the left.
   - B ☐ It is dangerous to walk on the right.
   - C ☐ Don't walk on this road.

4. **London luxury flat!**
   Near Trafalgar Square for rent starting September 1.
   Please ring doorbell after 5 pm on weekdays only.
   - A ☐ Someone is selling a luxury flat near Trafalgar Square on September 1 at 5 pm.
   - B ☐ You cannot get information about the luxury flat on weekends.
   - C ☐ You must move out of the luxury flat by September 1 at 5 pm.

15

# BEFORE YOU READ

## 1 VOCABULARY

**Match the words with their meaning.**

1 ☐ scary
2 ☐ mourner
3 ☐ jealous
4 ☐ confused
5 ☐ funeral

A feeling angry because you want to be like another person or have what that person has
B something that makes you afraid
C a religious function when a person dies
D when you feel you don't understand something
E a person who cries during a ceremony when somebody dies

PET

## 2 LISTENING

**Listen to Chapter Two and choose the correct answer — A, B or C.**

track 04

1 What did Mrs Sowerberry say about Oliver?
 A ☐ She said that he was pale and thin.
 B ☐ She said that he was ugly.
 C ☐ She said that he was good-looking.

2 Where did Oliver sleep the first night?
 A ☐ On the floor with the dog.
 B ☐ On the floor with the coffins.
 C ☐ In a warm, comfortable bed.

3 What was Noah Claypole like?
 A ☐ unfriendly
 B ☐ polite
 C ☐ friendly

4 How old was Oliver?
 A ☐ eleven
 B ☐ ten
 C ☐ nine

5 What did Noah say about Oliver's mother?
 A ☐ He said that she was a bad woman.
 B ☐ He said that she was a poor woman.
 C ☐ He said that she was an ugly woman.

CHAPTER **TWO**

# Mr Sowerberry's Shop

Mr Bumble and Oliver entered Mr Sowerberry's shop.

'Good Evening,' said Mr Bumble. 'Here's the boy, Mr Sowerberry.'

Mr Sowerberry turned around and looked at Oliver. Then he called his wife who was quite surprised and disappointed when she saw Oliver.

'Oh dear, this boy is very small,' she said, looking at the thin, pale boy who was standing in front of her.

'Yes, he's small but children grow, you know,' said Mr Bumble, smiling.

'Children grow if you give them food to eat,' said Mrs Sowerberry. 'This boy is going to cost us a lot of money; he looks hungry. Well, the dog isn't here tonight so you can eat his food. There are some pieces of cold meat.'

Oliver's eyes shone at the thought of meat and he ate the dog's food quickly and happily.

# Oliver Twist

'Now come with me,' said Mrs Sowerberry. 'I'll take you to your bed. It's in the shop. You can sleep there with the coffins. Good night.'

Oliver was alone in a dark room with a lot of coffins, and he was terribly afraid. His heart was beating [1] fast.

'What a scary place,' he thought, looking at all the coffins. 'I wonder if they're all empty.'

He felt alone in the world, without any parents or friends. He was very tired and after some time he fell asleep on the cold floor.

The next morning Oliver woke up and heard a loud noise outside the shop door. Someone was kicking the door.

A loud voice shouted, 'Open this door!'

Oliver went to the door and opened it. He saw a big boy with small eyes and a red nose standing in front of him.

'Are you the new boy?' he asked.

'Yes sir,' replied Oliver timidly.

'How old are you?' he asked.

'I'm ten, sir,' said Oliver.

'Well, I'm Mr Noah Claypole,' said the boy proudly. 'You work under me, is that clear? Now open the windows immediately!'

Noah was an unfriendly boy and he didn't like Oliver. He was jealous of Oliver and he often pulled his hair and his ears.

Oliver worked hard because there was a lot of work to do in Mr Sowerberry's shop. There were quite a lot of funerals.

One day Mr Sowerberry said to his wife, 'Oliver has such a sad face, he could be a good mourner.'

'You're right, dear,' said his wife. 'He'd be perfect with his thin, pale face.'

1. **beating** : (here) moving.

# Oliver Twist

So Mr Sowerberry gave Oliver a special black hat and a black jacket and he became a mourner at funerals.

After the first funerals Mr Sowerberry asked Oliver, 'Do you like funerals?'

'Not very much, sir,' said Oliver politely. However, Oliver continued to work as a mourner.

One day while they were working Noah started to ask questions about Oliver's mother and her death in the workhouse. He said that she was probably some kind of criminal.

Oliver's face became red with anger and he said, 'Don't say those things about my mother!'

'I can say whatever I want,' replied Noah, laughing. 'Your mother was a bad woman who died in a workhouse!'

Oliver was furious and he started hitting Noah hard. Noah was much bigger than Oliver, but Oliver wasn't afraid of him.

'Help!' cried Noah, who was really frightened. 'Someone help me! He's killing me!' Oliver continued to hit him and couldn't stop.

Mrs Sowerberry and a servant heard Noah and ran to the kitchen.

'What's going on in here?' cried Mrs Sowerberry, looking at the two boys who were fighting.

'Let's stop them.' said the servant, trying to separate the two boys.

The servant and Mrs Sowerberry stopped Oliver and started to hit him. Then they locked him in a small, dark room.

'Listen Noah,' said Mrs Sowerberry, 'go and call Mr Bumble, quickly!'

Noah ran out of the shop and went to look for Mr Bumble.

'Mr Bumble, sir,' cried Noah, 'something terrible has just happened! Oliver wanted to kill me and Mrs Sowerberry. Please come with me and help us!'

# Mr Sowerberry's Shop

When Mr Bumble and Noah got to the shop, Mr Bumble cried, 'Oliver!'

'Open the door!' shouted Oliver angrily. 'I want to get out of this dark room.'

'Do you know this voice, Oliver?' asked Mr Bumble.

'Yes, Mr Bumble, I do,' answered Oliver.

'Aren't you afraid, Oliver?' asked Mr Bumble.

'No, I'm not!' said Oliver in a brave voice.

'What!' said Mr Bumble, who was surprised. 'You're not afraid?'

'He's mad' said Mrs Sowerberry.

'No, he's not mad,' said Mr Bumble. 'it's the meat!'

'What do you mean?' asked Mrs Sowerberry, who was confused.

'You gave him too much meat to eat, Mrs Sowerberry,' said Mr Bumble. 'Meat makes them strong. At the workhouse we always give them porridge, and this never happens!'

'Oh dear, I was too kind to that bad boy!' said Mrs Sowerberry.

Mr Sowerberry came home later that evening and Mrs Sowerberry told him what happened. He went to the dark room and hit Oliver too, but he forgot to lock the door.

Poor Oliver spent a terrible night on the cold floor of the dark room. He cried all night and couldn't stop. He cried too many tears for a little boy. Early the next morning he saw that the door wasn't locked and so he decided to run away. He put a few clothes and a pair of socks in a handkerchief [2] and left Mr Sowerberry's shop. It was a cold morning and he didn't know where he was going, but he knew he had to leave that terrible place.

2. handkerchief :

# UNDERSTANDING THE TEXT

### 1 COMPREHENSION CHECK
Read the sentences below and choose the correct answer – A, B, C or D.

1 Mrs Sowerberry was surprised and disappointed to see Oliver
  - A ☐ because she didn't like boys.
  - B ☐ because he was very small and thin.
  - C ☐ but she smiled and gave him a kiss.
  - D ☐ and she sent him away with Mr Bumble.

2 Oliver was very glad because
  - A ☐ he was hungry and he could eat the dog's cold meat.
  - B ☐ he could sleep near the dog.
  - C ☐ he liked Mr and Mrs Sowerberry.
  - D ☐ he could sleep in Mr Sowerberry's shop.

3 Noah Claypole, who worked in the shop,
  - A ☐ was Mr Sowerberry's young cousin.
  - B ☐ was a mourner at funerals.
  - C ☐ kicked the door of the shop and woke Oliver up.
  - D ☐ became Oliver's best friend.

4 Oliver started to fight with Noah Claypole
  - A ☐ because Noah said bad things about his mother.
  - B ☐ since they had nothing to do in the morning.
  - C ☐ because Noah stole Oliver's black hat.
  - D ☐ because Noah said bad things about Mr Bumble.

5 Mr Bumble told Mrs Sowerberry that
  - A ☐ porridge made boys strong.
  - B ☐ meat made boys strong.
  - C ☐ meat made boys ill.
  - D ☐ Oliver didn't have enough to eat.

6 Who hit Oliver when he was locked in the small dark room?
  - A ☐ Mr Bumble and Mrs Sowerberry.
  - B ☐ Noah Claypole and the servant.
  - C ☐ The servant, Mrs Sowerberry and Mr Sowerberry.
  - D ☐ Mr Sowerberry.

## 2 SENTENCE TRANSFORMATION

For each question complete the second sentence so that it means the same as the first. Use no more than three words. The first is done for you.

0   It was too cold to work in the garden.
    It wasn't warm ..... *enough* ........... to work in the garden.

1   Oliver heard nothing when he was in the small dark room.
    Oliver ......................... anything when he was in the small dark room.

2   There were only a few children in the workhouse.
    There weren't ......................... in the workhouse.

3   Mr Sowerberry didn't live far from the church.
    Mr Sowerberry ......................... the church.

4   Meat was the food Oliver liked best.
    Oliver's ......................... meat.

5   Mr Bumble received a long letter from Mr Sowerberry.
    Mr Sowerberry ......................... a long letter.

6   Mr Bumble was very unpopular with everyone.
    No one ......................... Mr Bumble.

## 3 VOCABULARY

Complete the table with the missing noun or adjective.

|    | NOUN | ADJECTIVE |
|----|------|-----------|
| 1  | sleep | ......................... |
| 2  | ......................... | friendly |
| 3  | thirst | ......................... |
| 4  | ......................... | happy |
| 5  | anger | ......................... |
| 6  | ......................... | interesting |
| 7  | health | ......................... |
| 8  | ......................... | sad |
| 9  | beauty | ......................... |
| 10 | ......................... | hungry |

# BEFORE YOU READ

## 1 VOCABULARY

**Match the word with the correct picture.**

1 Milestone   2 Inn   3 Jewels   4 Wallet

A

B

C

D

PET

## 2 LISTENING

**Listen to the first part of Chapter Three and choose the correct answer — A, B or C.**

1 Mr Bumble could never find Oliver in London
   - A ☐ because London was far away.
   - B ☐ because London was a very big city.
   - C ☐ because there were many young boys there.
2 What did Oliver and the Dodger do at the inn?
   - A ☐ They slept because they were very tired.
   - B ☐ They talked to some old men.
   - C ☐ They ate some food.
3 Where did Fagin live?
   - A ☐ in the inn
   - B ☐ in an old, black house
   - C ☐ in the country
4 What did Fagin give Oliver?
   - A ☐ some bread and milk
   - B ☐ some warm food
   - C ☐ some pieces of cold meat
5 What was inside Fagin's secret box?
   - A ☐ a lot of money
   - B ☐ jewels and watches
   - C ☐ handkerchiefs and money

CHAPTER **THREE**

# Oliver Walks to London

Oliver walked and walked for a very long time. At about eight o'clock in the morning he was terribly tired and he decided to sit down near a milestone to rest. He looked at the milestone which said: LONDON 70 miles. [1]

'London! What a big city!' he thought. 'Mr Bumble certainly can't find me in a big city like London! Some old men at the workhouse said that a young boy can easily find work there. I've never seen a city. That's where I'll go!' Although he was still tired and hungry, he got up and started walking again. Now he knew where he was going and this made him feel better.

Oliver walked about twenty miles the first day and ate only one piece of dry bread with some water. That night he slept near the road. When he woke up the next morning he was terribly hungry and

1. **miles** : 1 mile = 1.6 kms.

# Oliver Twist

decided to buy some bread at the village bakery with his only penny. On that day he walked another twelve miles.

The next day a kind man gave him some bread and cheese, but as the days passed Oliver became very weak. A poor old lady gave him some food and water, but on the seventh day Oliver was exhausted.[2] He reached a little town near London and sat by the road to rest because his feet couldn't walk any further.

A strange boy with big ears and little eyes saw Oliver and said, 'Hello! What's the matter?' He was about Oliver's age but he was quite short and wore a long man's coat and a man's hat. Oliver looked up at the boy and told him his sad story.

The strange boy listened to his story and said, 'Don't worry! Come with me! I can help you.'

He took Oliver to an inn where they sat down and ate some bread and cold meat. The strange boy paid for the food.

'Thank you,' said Oliver, 'now I feel much better.'

The boy smiled and asked, 'Are you going to London?'

Oliver replied, 'Yes, I am.'

'Do you need a place to sleep?' asked the boy.

'Oh, yes I do!' said Oliver happily. 'I've slept outside in the cold and the rain for seven nights.'

'Stay with me!' said the boy. 'I know an old man in London and you can sleep at his house.'

'Really?' asked Oliver, who couldn't believe his ears.

'Yes, of course,' said the boy, calmly.

'You're very kind, thank you,' said Oliver smiling. 'What's your name?'

'My name's Jack Dawkins, but everyone calls me the artful Dodger,' said the boy. 'And what's your name?'

2. **exhausted** : very tired.

# Oliver Walks to London

'My name's Oliver Twist,' said Oliver. He felt that he had a friend. Together the two boys walked all the way to London.

When they arrived in London it was almost eleven o'clock and it was a cold, wet night. Oliver followed the Dodger through the narrow, dark streets. He looked at the old houses and saw that everything was dirty and ugly. There was an awful smell everywhere.

The Dodger stopped in front of an old, black house and opened the door. He and Oliver went up some broken stairs and then entered a dirty room with a lot of young boys. An ugly old man, with red hair and a red beard, was sitting near the fire. His clothes were old and dirty. He turned around and smiled at Oliver. 'Hello! I'm Fagin. Happy to meet you.'

'Good evening, sir. My name's Oliver Twist,' said Oliver, looking at all the handkerchiefs that were hanging in the room.

'We've just washed them,' said Fagin. 'I'm sure you're hungry. Sit down and eat some meat and bread.'

Oliver was happy to sit down at a table and eat some hot food in a warm room. Then Fagin showed him his bed and he soon fell asleep.

The next morning Oliver woke up while Fagin was preparing a cup of coffee for breakfast. Fagin turned around and looked at Oliver who closed his eyes and didn't move.

'Hmm, the boy is still asleep,' Fagin thought. He quietly took a box from a secret place under the floor. He put the box on the kitchen table and slowly opened it. He took out many splendid jewels and beautiful watches and looked at them, smiling. Then he suddenly turned around and saw that Oliver was awake. He immediately closed the box and said angrily, 'Why are you awake?'

'Oh, I'm sorry sir,' said Oliver, 'I've just opened my eyes.'

'Did you see those pretty things in the box?' asked Fagin, looking at Oliver.

# Oliver Twist

'Yes, sir, I did,' said Oliver.

'Well, you know, I'm an old man and they're all I have,' said Fagin, sadly. 'Now get up and go and wash your face. Then you can have breakfast with the other boys.'

Oliver got up and went to wash his face. 'Fagin must be a miser,[3] he thought. 'He lives in such an old, dirty place and yet he has so many jewels and watches.'

At that moment the Dodger and his friend Charley Bates arrived. They all sat down and had breakfast.

'Well, did you boys work hard this morning?' asked Fagin seriously.

'Yes, we did,' said the Dodger.

'Let's see!' said Fagin, smiling.

'Here are some wallets,' said the Dodger, putting them on the table.

'Are they full?' asked Fagin.

'Yes, they're nice and full,' said the Dodger proudly.

'And what about you, Charley?' said Fagin.

'Look, here are some good handkerchiefs,' said Charley Bates, putting them on the table next to the wallets.

'Good!' said Fagin smiling, 'you boys worked hard this morning.' Then he turned to Oliver and said, 'Well, Oliver, the Dodger and Charley are two good boys, aren't they?'

'Yes, sir, they certainly are,' said Oliver.

---

3. **miser** : a person who hates spending money and always saves it.

# UNDERSTANDING THE TEXT

### 1 COMPREHENSION CHECK

Read the passage below and choose the correct word for each space — A, B C or D. The first is done for you.

Oliver walked for a (0) ...C.... long time and was tired and hungry. He didn't know (1) .......... he was going, but when he saw the milestone which said London, he decided to walk there. He knew that Mr Bumble could (2) .......... find him in such a big city.

(3) .......... Oliver was resting by the side of the road he met a (4) .......... boy. The boy's name was Jack Dawkins, (5) .......... everyone called him the artful Dodger. They had some cold meat and bread at an inn and Dodger (6) .......... Oliver a place to stay in London. When they (7) .......... to London Oliver met an ugly old man called Fagin, (8) .......... lived in a dirty old house with (9) .......... young boys. One morning Oliver (10) .......... that Fagin had a secret box full of jewels and watches. During breakfast the Dodger and a friend called Charley Bates came home with some wallets and some nice handkerchiefs, which they gave to Fagin. He looked (11) .......... them and was happy with the boys' work.

| 0 | A much | B lots | C very | D so |
|---|---|---|---|---|
| 1 | A where | B what | C who | D which |
| 2 | A ever | B no | C none | D never |
| 3 | A And | B While | C So | D During |
| 4 | A stranger | B foreigner | C strange | D strangest |
| 5 | A because | B since | C for | D but |
| 6 | A offered | B invited | C took | D brought |
| 7 | A reached | B got | C arrived | D were |
| 8 | A that | B what | C how | D who |
| 9 | A lots | B a lot | C a lot of | D much |
| 10 | A saw | B looked | C watched | D identified |
| 11 | A to | B for | C at | D up |

## 'I'VE NEVER SEEN A CITY.'

We often use *ever/never* with the present perfect.

We use **ever** in questions. It means 'at any time up to now'.

*Has he **ever** been to London?*

*Never* means 'not ever' and we use it with a positive verb.

*We've **never** been to London.*

## 2 PRESENT PERFECT

**Complete the sentences with *ever* or *never*.**

1. Oliver has .................... been late to work.
2. Has she .................... studied French?
3. Mr Bumble has .................... been kind to anyone.
4. Have you .................... eaten porridge?
5. They have .................... lived in a workhouse.
6. I've .................... been to Turkey.
7. Have the children .................... played in the park?
8. Have we .................... played that game?

## 3 WRITING

Oliver wants to write to his friend James, who still lives in the workhouse. He wants to tell him about what happened at Mr Sowerberry's shop and why he left.

**Write a letter of approximately 100 words and tell James about:**

- Mr Sowerberry and his work
- Noah Claypole
- your decision to run away and go to London
- your first impression of London
- Fagin's house

**Start your letter like this:**

*Dear James,*
*I'm not working at Mr Sowerberry's shop any more. Let me tell you why...*

## 4 PREPOSITIONS

**Complete the sentences with the correct preposition from the box.**

> for    near    inside    on    at    under

1. The bread and meat were ............ Oliver, who was very hungry.
2. Oliver and Dodger had lunch ............ half past noon.
3. Oliver stood ............ a tall tree because it was raining hard.
4. Oliver sat ............ Dodger at the inn.
5. It was warm ............ Fagin's old flat.
6. There was a big market at the square ............ Saturday.

# BEFORE YOU READ

PET

### 1 LISTENING

**Listen to Chapter Four. Decide of each sentence is correct or incorrect. If it is correct, put a tick (✓) in the box under A for YES. If it is not correct, put a tick (✓) in the box under B for NO.**

|   |   | A | B |
|---|---|---|---|
| 1 | Oliver did not like the game Fagin, Charley Bates and the Dodger were playing. | ☐ | ☐ |
| 2 | Nancy and Bet were Fagin's two older daughters. | ☐ | ☐ |
| 3 | There were a lot of people at the market. | ☐ | ☐ |
| 4 | Dodger stole a handkerchief from an old man's pocket at the market. | ☐ | ☐ |
| 5 | Oliver did not want to be a thief. | ☐ | ☐ |
| 6 | The man who worked at the bookshop said that Oliver was not the thief. | ☐ | ☐ |
| 7 | Oliver felt weak and fell to the ground. | ☐ | ☐ |
| 8 | The policeman called a carriage and took Oliver home because he was not feeling well. | ☐ | ☐ |
| 9 | Mr Brownlow lived in an old, broken house. | ☐ | ☐ |
| 10 | Fagin and his friend Bill Sikes did not want to look for Oliver. | ☐ | ☐ |

### 2 READING PICTURES

**Look at the picture on page 35 and answer the following questions.**

1 Describe the scene and the people. Where are they? What are they doing?
2 What is Oliver thinking?
3 Who is stealing the handkerchief?
4 What do you think is going to happen?

CHAPTER **FOUR**

# Fagin's Strange Game

After breakfast Fagin, Charley Bates and the Dodger started playing a strange game which Oliver didn't understand. Fagin put a watch, a wallet, some handkerchiefs and some money in his pocket. Then he walked around the big room. Charley Bates and the Dodger followed him silently.

Fagin stopped sometimes and said, 'I'm talking to a friend,' or 'Now I'm looking at a shop window.' The two boys moved quickly and quietly and took the things from his pockets.

'Very good! Well done!' said Fagin, or, 'No! No! I felt that! Try again!'

They played the game many times and Oliver watched it and laughed. He wanted to play, too.

'Well, Oliver, do you want to play this game?' asked Fagin.

'Oh, yes, please,' Oliver said happily. Soon he played the game very well.

'You're a good boy, Oliver,' said Fagin. 'You play really well.'

Suddenly someone knocked at the door. Fagin opened it; there were two young ladies who came to visit Charley Bates and the Dodger. One was called Nancy and the other was Bet. They had long hair and wore dirty dresses.

# Oliver Twist

One morning after breakfast Fagin said to Oliver, 'Today you can go out with the Dodger and Charley Bates.'

'Oh, thank you, sir!' exclaimed Oliver. He was excited because he wanted to go out with his friends and work.

He followed the two boys to the market where people were working and selling all kinds of things. The three boys walked around very slowly, looking at the people.

The Dodger suddenly stopped and said softly, 'Be quiet! Look at that old man who's standing near the bookshop. He's perfect.'

The old man was well-dressed and he was looking at the bookshop window. The Dodger and Charley Bates went behind him silently. The Dodger put his hand in the old man's pocket and pulled out a lovely handkerchief. Then he gave it to Charley Bates and they both ran away quickly.

Oliver watched the two boys carefully and immediately understood the strange game. He also understood the mystery of Fagin's handkerchiefs, watches and jewels.

'Fagin and the boys are thieves!' he thought. 'I don't want to be a thief.'

He felt afraid and began to run away. At that moment the old man put his hand in his pocket and couldn't find his handkerchief.

'Stop, thief!' cried the old man turning around. 'A thief has stolen my handkerchief!'

The people near him started shouting, 'Stop, thief! Stop thief!'

The Dodger and Charley Bates also shouted, 'Stop thief!' Everyone started running after poor Oliver.

Oliver ran and then fell. A policeman caught him and shouted, 'Get up, thief!'

'I didn't steal the handkerchief!' said Oliver. 'Two other boys stole it, but they ran away. I'm not a thief!'

'*You're* the thief!' said the policeman angrily.

# Oliver Twist

'No! Stop!' said another man. 'I work at the bookshop and I saw what happened. This boy isn't a thief. Two other boys stole the handkerchief and ran away.'

'Please don't hurt the boy,' said the old man to the policeman. 'Let him go.'

Oliver was free, but he was frightened and weak. Suddenly he fell to the ground.

The old man was very kind and said, 'The poor boy! Look at his thin, pale face. He's not feeling well; he's probably hungry. He can come home with me.'

He called a carriage and took Oliver to his house. The kind old man's name was Mr Brownlow; he lived in a beautiful house with a garden in a quiet London street.

The Dodger and Charley Bates ran home; they were frightened.

'Well,' said Fagin, 'what happened? Where's Oliver?'

'A policeman took him away,' said the Dodger.

'What!' cried Fagin, who was furious. 'Now Oliver will tell the police about us and what we do. We must find him!'

At that moment a big man with dirty clothes opened the door and came in. He was about thirty-five years old and had angry eyes. His name was Bill Sikes and was Fagin's good friend. An old dog followed him.

'Well, Mr Sikes, you're angry today,' said Fagin. 'Tell me why.'

Sikes sat down at the kitchen table and took off his old coat. 'Give me something to drink, Fagin,' he said angrily.

Fagin gave Sikes something to drink and sat down next to him. He told Sikes about Oliver, and both men were worried. Sikes thought for a moment and said, 'We must find that boy, and I have a good plan. Listen!'

# UNDERSTANDING THE TEXT

## 1 COMPREHENSION CHECK

Match the phrases 1-9 to the phrases A-L to make complete sentences about Chapter Four. There are three phrases you will not need to use.

1. ☐ Fagin, Charley Bates and the Dodger played
2. ☐ There were handkerchiefs, a watch, a wallet and some money
3. ☐ Oliver watched the game and laughed
4. ☐ Nancy and Bet did not have
5. ☐ Oliver was happy and excited
6. ☐ The Dodger stole an old man's handkerchief
7. ☐ Everyone thought that Oliver
8. ☐ Mr Brownlow decided to
9. ☐ Fagin did not want

A but he didn't understand it.
B when Fagin told him to go out with the Dodger and Charley Bates.
C but he didn't want to play it.
D and his wallet.
E a strange game after breakfast.
F help Oliver and took him home in a carriage.
G and gave it to Charley Bates.
H in Fagin's pocket.
I nice clothes.
J Oliver to tell the police about him and what he did.
K send Oliver to prison.
L was the thief.

T : GRADE 4

## 2 SPEAKING - WORK

In Chapter Four there are many people in the market who are working. Talk to your partner about the kind of work you would like to do in the future. Use these questions to help you.

1. What kind of work do you like? Why?
2. Which school can prepare you for this kind of work?
3. How would you describe this kind of work: exciting, interesting, dangerous, boring, fun?

## 3 QUESTION WORDS

Complete the questions with *why*, *what*, *who*, *how* or *where*, and then choose the correct answer below.

1 .................... did Fagin, the Dodger and the other boys live?
2 .................... was Mr Bumble?
3 .................... did Oliver ask the cook at the workhouse?
4 .................... did Oliver fight Noah Claypole?
5 .................... did Oliver get to London?

A  He was an important officer in town.
B  Because he said bad things about his mother.
C  They lived in an old house in London.
D  He walked and walked for a long time.
E  He wanted another bowl of porridge.

**PET**

## 4 LISTENING

track 07

Listen to the information about the early history of London. Choose the correct answer — A, B or C.

1  Who sent an army to conquer Britain in the year 43 CE?
   A ☐ Emperor Constantine III
   B ☐ Tacitus
   C ☐ Emperor Claudius

2  How many soldiers were in this army?
   A ☐ 4,000 soldiers
   B ☐ 40,000 soldiers
   C ☐ 400 soldiers

3  Why did Londinium become an important town?
   A ☐ Because the emperor lived there.
   B ☐ Because of its geographic position on the River Thames.
   C ☐ Because there were many beautiful homes and palaces.

4  Why was Rome in danger at the beginning of the fifth century?
   A ☐ Because people from northern Europe started to attack it.
   B ☐ Because people from Britannia started to attack it.
   C ☐ Because there was very little food for the people.

38

### 5 NOTICES

Read each notice. What does it say? Choose the best answer — A, B or C.

**1**

**CAUTION!**
Broken bridge across the River Thames.
No one allowed beyond this point.

A ☐ People must not go any further.
B ☐ People must proceed with caution.
C ☐ If you want to see the River Thames you must go beyond this point.

**2**

BIG REWARD!
☞ 50 pounds ☜
For any information about the thief Fagin, last seen near London Bridge.

A ☐ Fagin will give you 50 pounds for any information about London Bridge.
B ☐ Fagin will receive 50 pounds for any information about London Bridge.
C ☐ You will receive 50 pounds for any information about Fagin.

**3**

TRAINS FOR LONDON
On rainy days trains for London leave from platform 2 instead of platform 5

A ☐ On sunny days go to platform 5 if you're going to London.
B ☐ Don't use platform 5 if you're going to London.
C ☐ When it rains you cannot use platforms 2 and 5.

**4**

THE LONDON THEATRE
Tickets are still available for the Tuesday performance of Shakespeare's
HAMLET
*Ticket office open every afternoon except weekends.*

A ☐ You can see a performance of HAMLET this weekend.
B ☐ You can't buy a ticket for the Tuesday performance on Saturday afternoon.
C ☐ You can buy a ticket for the Tuesday performance any weekday morning.

**5**

WANTED
Qualified young men who want to join London's Police Force.
*Must be strong and have at least three years experience as guards.*

A ☐ The London Police Force is looking for guards.
B ☐ Policemen must work three years for the London Police.
C ☐ You must be strong and qualified to join the London Police.

A group of poor orphans.

# Crime in Victorian London

There was a lot of poverty in 19th century Victorian London and a lot of crime. The city was crowded and criminals could hide easily. At night the dark, narrow streets were dangerous because there was very little light.

Poor children like Oliver Twist and the Dodger picked pockets and stole from street markets. Young thieves often worked together in teams and went to steal in rich homes and warehouses.[1] Young women, like Nancy, went to steal things in shops; they were called shoplifters.

There was a lot of violent crime in London too. In the late 1880s the terrible murders of Jack the Ripper, who killed several women in the

1. **warehouse** : a big building were products are kept.

Whitechapel area of London, shocked the people of London. The police were never able to find this murderer.

In 1829 Sir Robert (Bobby) Peel (1788-1850) started the London Metropolitan Police at Scotland Yard. It was the first modern police force in the world with about one thousand men. The police wore uniforms and were known as 'bobbies' or 'peelers', both because of Robert Peel's name. Their work was to stop crime in London's streets, which wasn't easy. Sir Robert Peel ordered his men to be courteous with everyone.

The people of London didn't like the police at first. But when there was less crime and the streets were safer, they began to understand the importance of the police. After 1856 there were police forces all over Great Britain.

The London Metropolitan Police Force became a model for the New York City Police in 1850 and for other police forces around the world.

In 1842 the first detective department was created at Scotland Yard. Detectives didn't wear uniforms and they investigated more complicated crimes. Today when we talk about the London Metropolitan Police we say 'Scotland Yard'– a name that is famous around the world.

### 1 COMPREHENSION CHECK
**Answer the following questions.**

1. What were Victorian London's streets like?
2. What did shoplifters do?
3. Why did Jack the Ripper shock the people of London?
4. The London Metropolitan Police Force became a model for which city?
5. Why were the first police called 'bobbies' or 'peelers'?
6. What did the first detectives at Scotland Yard do?

English 'Bobby' escorting two children.

# BEFORE YOU READ

PET

## 1 LISTENING

Listen to Chapter Five and choose the correct answer — A, B or C.

track 09

1  Who looked after Oliver?
- A ☐ Mr Brownlow
- B ☐ Mrs Bedwin
- C ☐ a doctor

2  Whose picture was on the wall near his bed?
- A ☐ the picture of a beautiful lady
- B ☐ the picture of Mr Brownlow's daughter
- C ☐ the picture of Mrs Bedwin's daughter

3  What did Mr Brownlow show Oliver?
- A ☐ his garden
- B ☐ his library
- C ☐ his sitting room

4  Where did Oliver meet Nancy?
- A ☐ at the bookshop
- B ☐ at the market
- C ☐ in a small, dark street

5  Who took Oliver's nice new clothes?
- A ☐ Fagin
- B ☐ Bill Sikes
- C ☐ Charley Bates

6  Who took Oliver's books?
- A ☐ Fagin
- B ☐ Charley Bates
- C ☐ Bill Sikes

7  What did Sikes do to Nancy when he got angry?
- A ☐ He pushed her to the floor.
- B ☐ He locked her in a small, dark room.
- C ☐ He hit her with a stick.

CHAPTER **FIVE**

# Mr Brownlow

When the carriage got to Mr Brownlow's home, Oliver could hardly walk because he was terribly weak and ill. Mr Brownlow immediately called his housekeeper.¹

'Mrs Bedwin! Come here please!'

'Yes, Mr Brownlow,' said Mrs Bedwin, who was a kind old woman.

'We must look after this poor young boy,' said Mr Brownlow. 'He's very ill. Let's put him in bed!'

'The poor child!' said Mrs Bedwin, looking at Oliver, who could hardly stand up.

Mr Brownlow and Mrs Bedwin took him to a sunny room and put him in a warm, clean bed. Oliver lay in bed for many days and Mrs Bedwin looked after him.

One morning Oliver opened his eyes and the first thing he saw

---

1. **housekeeper** : a person who looks after the house.

## Oliver Twist

was a picture of a beautiful lady on the wall near his bed. 'What a lovely lady!' said Oliver. 'But her eyes are very sad.'

One day Mr Brownlow came to Oliver's room and said, 'Well, dear boy, you're feeling a little bit better!'

Oliver was still weak but he smiled and said, 'Yes, sir, thank you! I'm a bit better.'

Mr Brownlow looked at the picture near Oliver's bed. He was silent for a moment and turned around and looked at Oliver. Then he looked at the picture again. He did this several times.

'Mrs Bedwin,' said Mr Brownlow, 'look at the picture on the wall and look at Oliver. Notice the head, the eyes, the mouth, the blonde hair – they're the same! I can't believe it!' He stared at the picture on the wall.

When Oliver was feeling better he got out of bed and sat on a chair in his room. Mr Brownlow often came to see him and talk to him. When he looked at Oliver he had tears in his eyes.

Many weeks passed and Oliver was finally better. Mr Brownlow and Mrs Bedwin loved little Oliver. Mr Brownlow bought him new clothes. Mrs Bedwin cooked him delicious meals, and for the first time in his life Oliver was happy. He had a family and a home.

'Oliver, are you happy here?' asked Mr Brownlow one day.

'I'm very happy here, sir,' said Oliver, smiling. 'You and Mrs Bedwin are so kind to me.'

'Do you want to stay here?' asked Mr Brownlow.

'Oh, yes!' exclaimed Oliver. 'Please don't send me away. I want to stay here always.'

'Good!' said Mr Brownlow happily. 'Come with me, Oliver. I want to show you my library.'

Oliver followed the old gentleman to his library, where there were hundreds of books on the bookshelves. Oliver was amazed.

# Oliver Twist

'I've never seen so many books,' said Oliver.

'I want to send you to a good school, Oliver,' said Mr Brownlow. 'You'll learn a lot of things and then you can read all these wonderful books.' Or perhaps you can become a writer!'

Oliver was surprised to hear this and looked at Mr Brownlow with big eyes. 'A writer, sir?'

'Yes, the author of a book!' exclaimed Mr Brownlow.

'Oh, Mr Brownlow, I would prefer to sell books rather than write them,' said Oliver.

Mr Brownlow laughed and looked kindly at Oliver.

'Very well, you can certainly sell books and not write them,' said Mr Brownlow.

'Oh, thank you, sir,' replied Oliver.

One day Mr Brownlow said, 'Oliver, can you please take these books to the bookshop? Give the man in the shop this £5 note.'[2]

'Of course, Mr Brownlow,' said Oliver, 'I'm happy to do it for you.' He put on his new coat and took the books and the £5 note. It was a sunny day and he walked happily down the street.

When Oliver turned into a small, dark street Nancy saw him and put her arms around him.

'My dear little brother!' said Nancy. 'I've found you! You must come home with me now. You're a bad boy! We were worried about you.'

'Help! Help!' cried poor Oliver, who didn't know what to do.

Just then Bill Sikes arrived and said, 'Come home with us, Oliver. Mother's waiting for you!'

Bill Sikes and Nancy pulled Oliver all the way to Fagin's house.

'Oliver!' exclaimed Fagin, 'I'm happy to see you!'

2. £5 :

Charley Bates took Oliver's nice new clothes, Fagin took the books and Sikes took the £5 note.

Oliver was very angry and said, 'You can keep me here all my life, but please return these books and the £5 note to Mr Brownlow. Please! He mustn't think I'm a thief.'

Everyone laughed at Oliver.

'Yes, Oliver,' said Fagin laughing, 'Mr Brownlow will think you're a thief!'

Oliver wanted to run away. He jumped up and ran to the door, but Fagin hit him with a big stick. Nancy took the stick out of Fagin's hand and threw it in the fire.

'Don't hit that poor boy again!' she said angrily.

Sikes got angry and pushed Nancy to the floor, while Fagin laughed. Then Fagin locked Oliver in a small, dark room. He remembered the small, dark room at Mr Sowerberry's shop; he started crying and was very unhappy.

'What will Mr Brownlow think? And Mrs Bedwin?' thought Oliver. 'What can I do now?'

Mr Brownlow and Mrs Bedwin waited for Oliver all day and all night, but he never came home. They were very worried.

'What has happened to Oliver?' said Mr Brownlow, looking at his watch sadly. 'Where is the poor boy?'

'Oh, Mr Brownlow,' said Mrs Bedwin, 'something terrible has probably happened to him.'

# UNDERSTANDING THE TEXT

## 1 COMPREHENSION CHECK

Read the sentences below and choose the correct answer — A, B, C or D.

1 Who was Mrs Bedwin?
   - A ☐ Mr Brownlow's sister
   - B ☐ Mr Brownlow's aunt
   - C ☐ Mr Brownlow's neighbour
   - D ☐ Mr Brownlow's housekeeper

2 Why did Mr Brownlow stare at the picture on the wall?
   - A ☐ Because the lady in the picture looked like Oliver.
   - B ☐ Because the lady in the picture was Mr Brownlow's daughter.
   - C ☐ Because the lady in the picture was Mrs Bedwin's daughter.
   - D ☐ Because the lady in the picture was Mr Brownlow's wife.

3 Where did Mr Brownlow send Oliver?
   - A ☐ He sent him to a good school.
   - B ☐ He sent him to the bookshop.
   - C ☐ He sent him to the bank with a £5 note.
   - D ☐ He sent him to the library.

4 What happened to Oliver while he was walking down the street?
   - A ☐ A thief stopped him and took the £5 note.
   - B ☐ He lost the books Mr Brownlow gave him.
   - C ☐ Nancy and Bill Sikes found him.
   - D ☐ He fell and hurt himself.

5 Why did Fagin hit Oliver with a big stick?
   - A ☐ Because Fagin didn't like Oliver.
   - B ☐ Because Oliver tried to run away.
   - C ☐ Because Oliver didn't want to give him the £5 note.
   - D ☐ Because Oliver started crying loudly.

## 'YOU AND MRS BEDWIN ARE THE KINDEST PEOPLE IN THE WORLD!' SAID OLIVER, SMILING.

**Kindest** is the superlative form of the adjective **kind**.

We form the superlative of adjectives like this:

with adjectives of one syllable we add **-est**:

old – **the oldest**          hot – **the hottest**          cold – **the coldest**

with adjectives of two or more syllables ending in -**y**, we change the *y* to *i* and add -**est**:
*happy* – **happiest**     *lucky* - **luckiest**

with adjectives of two or more syllables, we use most before the adjective:
*beautiful* – **the most beautiful**     *important* – **the most important**

some adjectives have an irregular superlative:
*good* – **the best**     *bad* – **the worst**     *far* – **the farthest/furthest**

## 2 SUPERLATIVES

**Complete the sentences with the superlative form of the adjective in brackets.**

1 The workhouse was .................... experience Oliver ever had. (difficult)
2 Oliver was .................... boy in the workhouse. (sad)
3 Yesterday's storm was .................... of the year. (bad)
4 James was .................... boy at the orphanage. (nice)
5 Charles Dickens was .................... writer of the Victorian Age. (famous)
6 Mr Brownlow went to .................... bookshop in London. (expensive)
7 Mrs Bedwin had .................... room in the house. (big)
8 Saturday was .................... day of the week. (sunny)

## 3 SCRAMBLED WORD CLOZE

**Oliver wants to tell Mr Brown what happened to him. Complete the letter with the words from the box.**

| brother | thief | money | clothes | frightened | anything | bad |
| arms | bookshop | dark | him | books | terrible | Fagin's |

Dear Mr Brownlow,

Something (**1**) .................... happened to me while I was going to the (**2**) .................... . When I turned into a (**3**) .................... street, I suddenly saw Nancy. She put her (**4**) .................... around me and said, 'My dear little (**5**) ....................! I found you!' I cried out but no one heard me. I couldn't do (**6**) .................... because Bill Sikes arrived. He's a very (**7**) .................... man and I don't like (**8**) .................... . Nancy and Sikes pulled me all the way to (**9**) .................... house and I was very (**10**) .................... . Fagin took the (**11**) ...................., Sikes took the (**12**) .................... and Charley Bates took my new (**13**) .................... . I'm sorry, Mr Brownlow. Please believe me, I'm not a (**14**) ....................!

Your friend,

Oliver

# BEFORE YOU READ

### 1 LISTENING

Listen to the first part of Chapter Six and choose the correct answer — A, B or C.

1 What was the weather like when Fagin went to see Bill Sikes?

2 What did Oliver find near his bed one morning?

3 What did Sikes put to Oliver's head?

4 What time was it?

CHAPTER **SIX**

# A Terrible Night

One stormy night someone knocked at Bill Sikes's door; it was Fagin.

'Listen, Sikes, I want to talk to you about that big house outside London.'

'Do you mean that big, rich house with the garden?' asked Sikes.

'Yes,' said Fagin. 'That house belongs to a very rich family, and there are a lot of valuable [1] things to steal. It's perfect for us!'

'Well, it won't be easy,' said Sikes nervously. 'I've already seen that house; it's completely closed at night. There's only one very small window at the back. It's easy to open, but only a small, thin boy can enter.'

'Exactly!' exclaimed Fagin. 'And I have the right boy!'

'Who's the right boy?' asked Sikes.

'Oliver's the boy for you, Sikes,' said Fagin. 'He's small and thin, and he must start working for his bread.'

1. **valuable** : worth a lot of money.

# Oliver Twist

'What about the other boys?' asked Sikes.

'Charley Bates and the Dodger are too big; Oliver's the right size,' said Fagin.

'Alright, Fagin,' said Sikes. 'Will you talk to him?'

'Yes, I'll talk to him and tell him what to do,' said Fagin.

The next morning Oliver found a new pair of shoes near his bed, and he was happy.

'Well, Oliver, do you like your new shoes?' asked Fagin.

'Yes, sir, thank you!' said Oliver, putting them on.

'Tonight I have a job for you, Oliver,' said Fagin.

'A job for me?' asked Oliver timidly.

'Yes, for you,' said Fagin. 'Now listen very carefully. Tonight you'll go to see Bill Sikes.'

'Why?' asked Oliver, who didn't like Bill Sikes.

'Sikes will explain everything to you, but be careful,' said Fagin. 'Bill Sikes is a cruel man. Do exactly what he tells you. Do you understand, Oliver?'

'Yes, sir,' said Oliver, who didn't want to go to Sikes's house.

Soon Nancy came and took Oliver to Sikes.

'Be good and quiet, Oliver,' said Nancy, taking his hand. 'And listen to Sikes. Remember, he's a cruel man.'

When Sikes saw Oliver he put a pistol[2] to his head and said, 'Do what I say or I'll shoot you! Do you hear me?' Oliver was so terrified that he couldn't say a word. He looked at Sikes's ugly face and felt terrible.

'Now come with me!' said Sikes, pulling Oliver's arm. 'It's a quarter past midnight and time for us to work!'

It was cold and foggy as they walked through the dark, narrow

2. pistol :

# A Terrible Night

streets of London. After a long walk they got to the country. They met another thief called Toby Crackit. Oliver walked between the two thieves and they soon came to a garden wall. They climbed the wall and saw a big country house.

As soon as Oliver saw the big country house he understood their terrible plan. He fell to his knees and said, 'Please let me go! Please! I don't want to steal. I prefer to die here.'

Toby Crackit and Bill Sikes looked at each other nervously.

'Be quiet!' said Sikes angrily.

Toby put his hand over Oliver's mouth. They walked to the back of the house and Sikes opened the small window. He put a pistol to Oliver's head and whispered, 'Go in through this small window and then go to the front door. Open it and we'll come in. Remember, Oliver, I'm watching you… and I have a pistol!'

Oliver didn't have a choice. He had to do what Sikes told him. So he went in through the small window. When he was inside the house he wanted to warn the family so he started going up the stairs.

'What's that boy doing?' said Sikes, who was watching Oliver. 'Come back, Oliver!'

Suddenly there was a light. There were two men at the top of the stairs. One man had a light and the other had a pistol. There was a loud noise and smoke, and Oliver felt a terrible pain in his arm. He ran back to the small window.

Sikes put his arm through the window and pulled Oliver through the window.

'Oliver's badly hurt,' said Sikes. 'Look at the blood! Let's get out of here!'

He carried Oliver to the garden wall. Oliver was very cold and suddenly he couldn't see or hear anything.

'Hurry, Sikes!' cried Toby Crackit. 'The men are following us with their dogs!'

Sikes left poor Oliver at the garden wall and ran away with Toby Crackit. The two men were servants and they followed Sikes and Toby Crackit.

'It's dark and foggy,' said Mr Brittles. 'Can you see anyone, Giles?'

'No, it's too dark. I can't see anything,' said Mr Giles.

'Well, let's go back then,' said Mr Brittles.

The two men turned around and walked back to the country house. It was so dark that they didn't see Oliver's body near the garden wall. He stayed on the cold, wet ground all night.

# UNDERSTANDING THE TEXT

## 1 COMPREHENSION CHECK

Read the text below and choose the correct word for each space — A, B, C or D. The first is done for you.

Fagin (0) ......B........ on Bill Sikes's door one stormy night (1) ............... he wanted to talk to him about a big rich house (2) ............... London. Fagin wanted to steal things from that house. Sikes said he knew the house, but it was (3) ............... difficult to enter. Fagin said that Oliver was the (4) ............... boy for the job since he was small and thin. Sikes (5) ............... to the plan and Fagin went back home.

The next morning Fagin put a new pair of shoes near Oliver's bed and (6) ............... him that there was a (7) ............... for him. That night Oliver followed Sikes all the way to the country, (8) ............... they met Toby Crackit, another thief. Together they went to the big house and climbed the garden wall.

Oliver did not want to steal from the big house, but he had no (9) ............... . When Oliver was inside the house he tried to (10) ............... the family and went up the stairs. Suddenly one man at the top of the stairs shot Oliver with his pistol. Oliver was (11) ............... hurt and ran back to the small window and escaped. Sikes carried poor Oliver to the garden wall and left him there.

| 0 | A | hit | (B) | knocked | C | beat | D | touched |
|---|---|---|---|---|---|---|---|---|
| 1 | A | that | B | so | C | how | D | because |
| 2 | A | out | B | outskirts | C | outside | D | far |
| 3 | A | much | B | lots | C | very | D | many |
| 4 | A | correct | B | right | C | write | D | perfectly |
| 5 | A | agreed | B | agreement | C | agree | D | agreeing |
| 6 | A | said | B | talked | C | spoke | D | told |
| 7 | A | work | B | project | C | job | D | position |
| 8 | A | that | B | where | C | how | D | since |
| 9 | A | choice | B | choose | C | chose | D | chosen |
| 10 | A | say | B | warn | C | caution | D | speak |
| 11 | A | bad | B | much | C | many | D | badly |

## 2 CROSSWORD

Complete the crossword below.

### ACROSS

3
6  A child without parents.
8  A person who steals things.
10 A place where very poor people live.
11 A person who doesn't understand something.
12
13

### DOWN

1  Children without a family live here.
2
4  It makes you afraid.
5
7  Warm breakfast food made with cereal and milk or water.
9  A person who looks after a house.

## 3 CHARACTERS

**Write a short description of each of the characters below using some of the words in the box below. You can use the same words more than once.**

kind   honest   young   evil   friendly   cruel   thin   tall
angry   poor   alone   sad   lucky   miser   terrified

**Oliver**

..................................
..................................
..................................
..................................

**Fagin**

..................................
..................................
..................................
..................................

**Sikes**

..................................
..................................
..................................
..................................

**the Dodger**

..................................
..................................
..................................
..................................

**Nancy**

..................................
..................................
..................................
..................................

**Mr Brownlow**

..................................
..................................
..................................
..................................

CHAPTER **SEVEN**

# Oliver's New Home

When Oliver woke up the next morning it was raining hard and the sky was dark. He was very weak and his left arm hurt terribly. He looked at it and saw that it was covered with blood. From the garden wall he could see the big country house.

'Perhaps the people in that house can help me,' he thought.

He got up and slowly walked to the house. He knocked at the door and fell to the ground.

Mr Giles and Mr Brittles heard the knock and opened the door.

'Oh dear!' exclaimed Mr Giles. 'It's a boy!'

Then he saw the blood on Oliver's clothes and said, 'It's one of the thieves!' He went to the sitting room to tell the ladies.

'The thief I shot last night is here!' said Mr Giles. 'Do you want to see him?'

'The thief from last night? Oh no, not now,' said Rose Maylie, who was a beautiful girl of seventeen with a friendly smile. She had blonde

# Oliver Twist

hair and blue eyes, and wore lovely clothes. She lived with her aunt, Mrs Maylie.

'Please take him upstairs to your room, Mr Giles,' said Rose Maylie. 'Tell Mr Brittles to go to town and ask Doctor Losberne to come here immediately.'

When Dr Losberne arrived he said, 'What happened last night? Mr Brittles said there were thieves in the house.'

'Yes, there were,' said Rose Maylie, 'but luckily they ran away when Mr Giles shot one of them.'

'Oh dear! Are you ladies alright?' asked Doctor Losberne, a tall man with dark hair.

'Yes, thank you, but please look at the thief upstairs,' said Rose. 'He was shot last night and he's hurt.'

'Of course, I'll look at him immediately,' said Doctor Losberne, going upstairs.

He stayed upstairs a long time and when he came down he said, 'Ladies, please come upstairs with me.'

Rose and her aunt, Mrs Maylie, followed the doctor upstairs and had a big surprise. They didn't see a bad thief in bed; they saw a little boy sleeping. They looked at him in silence. Rose sat down near the bed and had tears in her eyes.

'This poor little boy can't be a thief,' said Rose.

'Oh no,' said Mrs Maylie, looking at Oliver. 'He can't be a thief; he's so young.'

'He needs to rest now,' said Doctor Losberne. 'I looked at his arm and it'll get better soon. When he wakes up give him something to eat and milk to drink. The poor little boy is very thin and pale. I'll be back to see him tomorrow.'

'Thank you very much, Doctor Losberne,' said Rose and Mrs Maylie.

# Oliver's New Home

Later in the evening Oliver woke up after a long sleep and saw Rose sitting near his bed.

'Hello,' she said smiling at him. 'My name's Rose and you're in my house. Please don't be afraid; we want to help you.'

Oliver smiled at Rose and said, 'Thank you!'

He then told Rose the story of his sad life: the orphanage, the workhouse, Mr Sowerberry's shop, Fagin, Sikes and kind Mr Brownlow. He spoke slowly and softly because he was very weak and had a high temperature. He was ill for a long time and stayed in bed.

Doctor Losberne came to see Oliver every day and Rose and her aunt looked after him. They liked Oliver a lot and he slowly got better. He spent time in the garden and went for walks with Rose and Mrs Maylie. He listened to Rose play the piano and sing. And Rose often read stories to him.

After some time a teacher came to give Oliver lessons, which he liked very much. Three months passed and Oliver was very happy. He loved Rose and Mrs Maylie; they were his new family.

One day Oliver asked Rose and Mrs Maylie, 'What can I do for you? You were so kind to me when I was ill.'

Rose laughed and said. 'We love you Oliver, and we're very happy because you're here with us.'

In the summer Rose and Mrs Maylie took Oliver to their lovely cottage in the country. There were trees and flowers everywhere. Oliver liked working in the garden and soon became strong and healthy.

One day Oliver said, 'This is such a beautiful place. It's very different from the noisy city.'

'I'm glad you like our country cottage,' said Rose. 'We always come here in the summer.'

# Oliver Twist

At the end of the summer Oliver, Rose and Mrs Maylie returned home to London.

One afternoon Oliver was studying his lessons at his desk, which was next to a big window. When he looked out of the window, he saw two men in the garden. He recognized one of them immediately; it was Fagin. The other man was tall and had an angry face. He wore a black coat and a black cap.

'Oh, no!' thought Oliver. 'It's Fagin with another strange man.'

Fagin looked at the window and said to the other man, 'That's the boy, Monks. That's Oliver!'

'Yes, it's Oliver!' said Monks. 'We've found him. Now we know where he lives.'

Oliver saw them through the window. He was frightened and jumped up from his desk. Fagin and Monks ran away.

'Fagin!' Fagin!' cried Oliver. Two servants came into the room and said, 'Oliver, what's happening here? You look frightened.'

'I've just seen Fagin and another strange man,' Oliver said excitedly. 'They were in the garden and they saw me!' His face was white.

'Don't worry, Oliver!' said one of the servants. 'We'll go into the garden and find them!'

The two servants ran out into the garden and looked for the two men, but they couldn't find them.

# UNDERSTANDING THE TEXT

## 1 COMPREHENSION CHECK

Read the sentences below and decide if each sentence is correct or incorrect. If it is correct, put a tick (✓) in the box under A for YES. If it is not correct, put a tick (✓) in the box under B for NO.

                                                                                            A   B

1. When Oliver woke up he was lying near the garden wall.
2. Oliver's right leg was covered with blood and hurt terribly.
3. Mr Giles and Mr Brittles found Oliver near the garden wall and carried him to the big country house.
4. Oliver, who was very weak, was taken to Mr Giles room.
5. Mrs Maylie and Mr Brittles went to town to look for Doctor Losberne, who came immediately.
6. When Rose and her aunt saw the young thief they got angry with him.
7. During the summer Rose and her aunt took Oliver to their seaside cottage.
8. Oliver's desk was next to a big window.
9. Oliver was very frightened when he recognized Fagin in the garden outside the house.
10. Mr Giles and Mr Brittles found the two men and called the police.

## WHEN OLIVER WOKE UP THE NEXT MORNING IT WAS RAINING HARD AND THE SKY WAS DARK.

Time clauses are used to say when something happens by referring to a period of time or to another event.

Look at these examples:

*They ate lunch **while** they were travelling.*

*The children ran away **as soon as** they saw Mr Bumble.*

*Oliver went to the inn **before** it started raining.*

*He wrote to James **when** he reached London.*

## 2 TIME CLAUSES

Complete the following sentences with a time clause from the box below.

> while   after   before   as soon as   when   until

1 .................... having breakfast, Oliver always washed his hands.
2 Rose Maylie first talked to Mr Giles and .................... she called the doctor.
3 Fagin talked to Bill Sikes .................... midnight.
4 Oliver wanted to run away .................... he saw the big country house and understood Sikes's plan.
5 Oliver slept .................... Fagin was looking at his jewels.
6 .................... Rose Maylie saw Oliver sleeping, she had tears in her eyes.

## 3 WRITING

You are a young journalist who works for the London Gazette. You have to write an article of about 100 words about the attempted robbery at the Maylie home. Start like this:

*ROBBERY AT THE MAYLIE HOME*
*Last night a young thief entered the Maylie home while everyone was sleeping...*

## 4 SENTENCE TRANSFORMATION

For each question complete the second sentence so that it means the same as the first. Use no more than three words. The first is done for you.

0 Rose Maylie likes summer more than winter.
Rose Maylie ...prefers summer.... to winter.

1 Charley Bates isn't as tall as Bill Sikes.
Charley Bates is .............................. Bill Sikes.

2 'Shall we cross London Bridge?' said Oliver to the Dodger.
'Why .............................. cross London Bridge?' said Oliver to the Dodger.

3 It was so foggy we couldn't see the road.
It was too .............................. the road.

4 Fagin lived near the old bridge.
Fagin didn't live .............................. the old bridge.

# BEFORE YOU READ

**PET**

## 1 LISTENING

**Listen to Chapter Eight and choose the correct answer – A, B or C.**

track 12

1 How much money did Monks give Mr Bumble?
- A ☐ twenty-five pounds in gold
- B ☐ a twenty pound note
- C ☐ two big gold coins.

2 What did Mrs Bumble steal from Oliver's mother?
- A ☐ two gold coins
- B ☐ her gold wedding ring
- C ☐ her gold watch

3 Why did Nancy go to Fagin's house?
- A ☐ Because she wanted to see Oliver.
- B ☐ Because Sikes sent her.
- C ☐ Because Sikes was very ill.

4 Why was Nancy frightened?
- A ☐ Because Fagin was a bad man.
- B ☐ Because she heard some terrible things.
- C ☐ Because Sikes was angry with her.

5 Who is Monks?
- A ☐ Monks is Fagin's brother.
- B ☐ Monks is Bill Sikes's half-brother.
- C ☐ Monks is Oliver's half-brother.

6 What does Rose Maylie offer Nancy?
- A ☐ some money
- B ☐ a warm coat
- C ☐ a gold ring

7 Where and when will Nancy meet Rose Maylie?
- A ☐ at London Bridge on Sunday night
- B ☐ at London Park between eleven and midnight
- C ☐ at London Bridge on Sunday morning

CHAPTER **EIGHT**

# Nancy's Secret

After a few years Mr Bumble became the master of the workhouse where Oliver was born. He felt very important. One evening Monks went to the workhouse to talk to him.

'Are you Mr Bumble?' asked Monks.

'Yes, I'm the master of the workhouse,' said Mr Bumble proudly. 'Who are you?'

'My name is Monks.'

'What do you want?' asked Mr Bumble.

'Listen to me carefully,' said Monks, looking at Mr Bumble. 'You must tell me something important.' He put two big gold coins on the table. 'These gold coins are for you.'

Mr Bumble quickly put them in his pocket and smiled at Monks.

'What do you want to know?' said Mr Bumble.

'Twelve years ago a boy was born in your workhouse,' said Monks. 'His mother died immediately after he was born. Do you remember?'

67

# Oliver Twist

'Yes, I remember,' said Mr Bumble. 'Poor woman! That boy is Oliver Twist.'

'Your wife was with Oliver's mother when she died,' said Monks. 'Your wife took something from her.'

'What do you mean?' asked Mr Bumble, who was confused.

'I want to talk to your wife,' said Monks. 'Meet me at the old house near the river tomorrow night.'

'Alright,' said Mr Bumble. 'We'll meet you there at 8 o'clock, but remember to bring money. If you want information you have to pay for it.'

'Don't worry,' said Monks angrily. 'If your wife gives me the information I want, I'll give her lots of money.'

'My wife knows a lot of things,' said Mr Bumble.

The next night Mr and Mrs Bumble walked to the house near the river and waited for Monks.

When he arrived he said, 'Let's go inside this old house. No one lives here.'

They went into the house and sat down around a small wooden table. Monks lit a small candle. The three people looked at each other nervously.

'Now,' Monks said, looking at Mrs Bumble, 'you were with Oliver Twist's mother when she died, weren't you?'

'Yes, I was,' said Mrs Bumble. 'What do you want to know?'

'Tell me about Oliver Twist's mother,' said Monks.

Mrs Bumble was silent for a moment and then said, 'First give me twenty-five pounds in gold, and then I'll tell you all you want to know.'

'Alright,' said Monks and gave her the money. Mrs Bumble took it and told him that when Oliver's mother died, she stole her gold wedding ring.

# Nancy's Secret

'Show me the ring,' said Monks.

Mrs Bumble showed Monks a gold wedding ring which had a name inside: Agnes.

'This is the ring I want,' said Monks, putting the ring in his pocket. 'We can go now.'

That night Monks threw the gold wedding ring into the river and said angrily, 'No one can find it in the river! No one will ever know the truth.'

Bill Sikes was ill for several weeks and Nancy looked after him, because she loved him. One day when he was feeling better he said to Nancy, 'Go to Fagin and ask him for some money.'

Nancy went to Fagin's house and told him what Sikes wanted.

'Well, my friend Sikes wants some money,' said Fagin. 'Wait here, Nancy.'

While Nancy was waiting for Fagin, someone knocked at the door. It was Monks and he looked at Nancy because he didn't know her.

'Don't worry, Monks,' said Fagin. 'Nancy is one of my young people.'

'I want to talk to you privately about something important,' said Monks, nervously. 'Let's go into the other room.'

'Alright,' said Fagin, 'follow me.'

Fagin and Monks went to the other room and shut the door. But Nancy wanted to know what was happening, so she listened at the door. They were speaking softly but Nancy could hear everything they said; she heard some terrible things and was frightened.

'Tomorrow I must talk to Rose Maylie,' thought Nancy. 'Oliver is in danger.'

When Monks left, Fagin gave Nancy some money and she went home to Sikes. Early the next morning she went to buy food and

# Oliver Twist

drink for him; he was still ill and in bed. He ate and drank a lot and fell asleep.

'Good! Sikes is sleeping,' thought Nancy. 'Now I can go.' She put on her coat and shut the door silently. Then she ran down the stairs and up the street. She ran across London to the Maylies' house. She knocked at the door and a servant opened the door.

'My name's Nancy and I want to see Miss Rose Maylie, please. It's very important.'

The servant looked at her old clothes and then went upstairs. When he returned he said, 'Please follow me.' As Nancy followed the servant to Rose's room, she looked at the lovely furniture and paintings on the walls.

'Hello, I'm Rose Maylie. You wanted to see me?'

Rose's gentle manner and sweet voice surprised Nancy, who started crying.

'Please sit down, miss,' said Rose gently. 'What's wrong? Why are you crying?'

'Dear lady,' said Nancy, looking at Rose, 'I came here to tell you a terrible secret.'

'A terrible secret?' asked Rose, who was surprised.

'Yes, a terrible secret,' said Nancy. 'Oliver Twist is in great danger and I want to save him!'

'Oliver!' exclaimed Rose.

'Yes, let me explain,' said Nancy. She told Rose about Fagin and Monks.

'Monks is a very bad man. He knows that Oliver lives here and he and Fagin want to kidnap[1] him. Fagin is a criminal who teaches boys to steal. Monks wants Oliver to become a thief. Then the police can

---

1. **kidnap** : take someone away with force, usually for money.

# Oliver Twist

catch him and put him in prison or kill him! Monks wants his brother to die!'

'His brother!' exclaimed Rose. 'What do you mean?'

'Yes,' said Nancy, 'Oliver is Monks's half brother. Last night I heard Monks say, "Nobody knows the name of Oliver's mother. I threw her gold wedding ring into the river." But I don't know all of his plan.'

'This is terrible! What can we do to help Oliver?' asked Rose, who was very worried.

'You must tell this secret to a good man who can help Oliver,' said Nancy.

'Yes, you're right,' said Rose. 'I think I know the right man. When can we meet again?'

Nancy thought for a moment and said, 'Meet me on London Bridge on Sunday night, between eleven and midnight.'

'Very well,' said Rose. 'Thank you for coming here, Nancy.'

'I must go now,' said Nancy.

'Oh, no!' said Rose. 'Please don't go back to those thieves and criminals. I can help you, Nancy. Take some money and go far away. You can start a new life far away from London.'

'You're very kind, dear lady,' said Nancy, 'but I don't want any money. No one can help me because it's too late. I don't have a future. Thank you for your kindness. Remember, Sunday night on London Bridge.'

'Yes, Sunday night then!' said Rose, smiling.

# UNDERSTANDING THE TEXT

## 1 COMPREHENSION CHECK

Match the phrases 1-12 to the phrases A-O to make complete sentences about Chapter Eight. There are three phrases you do not need to use.

1  ☐ Mr Bumble felt important
2  ☐ Monks told Mr Bumble that
3  ☐ Monks and Mr Bumble decided
4  ☐ Monks gave Mrs Bumble twenty-five pounds
5  ☐ Monks decided to throw
6  ☐ Bill Sikes was ill and sent Nancy
7  ☐ Nancy listened to Fagin and Monk's conversation
8  ☐ While Sikes was sleeping Nancy
9  ☐ Nancy told Rose that Monks
10 ☐ Rose and Nancy were very worried and
11 ☐ Fagin gave Nancy
12 ☐ Nancy said that

A  to meet at the old house near the river at eight o'clock.
B  the gold wedding ring into the river.
C  because he became the master of the workhouse.
D  to meet in London the next day.
E  went to the Maylie house.
F  to Fagin's house to ask for money.
G  to look for a doctor.
H  he wanted to talk to his wife.
I  wanted his brother to die.
J  and she gave him a gold wedding ring.
K  decided to meet Sunday night on London Bridge.
L  and heard some terrible things.
M  decided to go and talk to the police.
N  some money.
O  she does not have a future.

## 2 CHARACTERS
Look at the characters and write a brief description of each one.

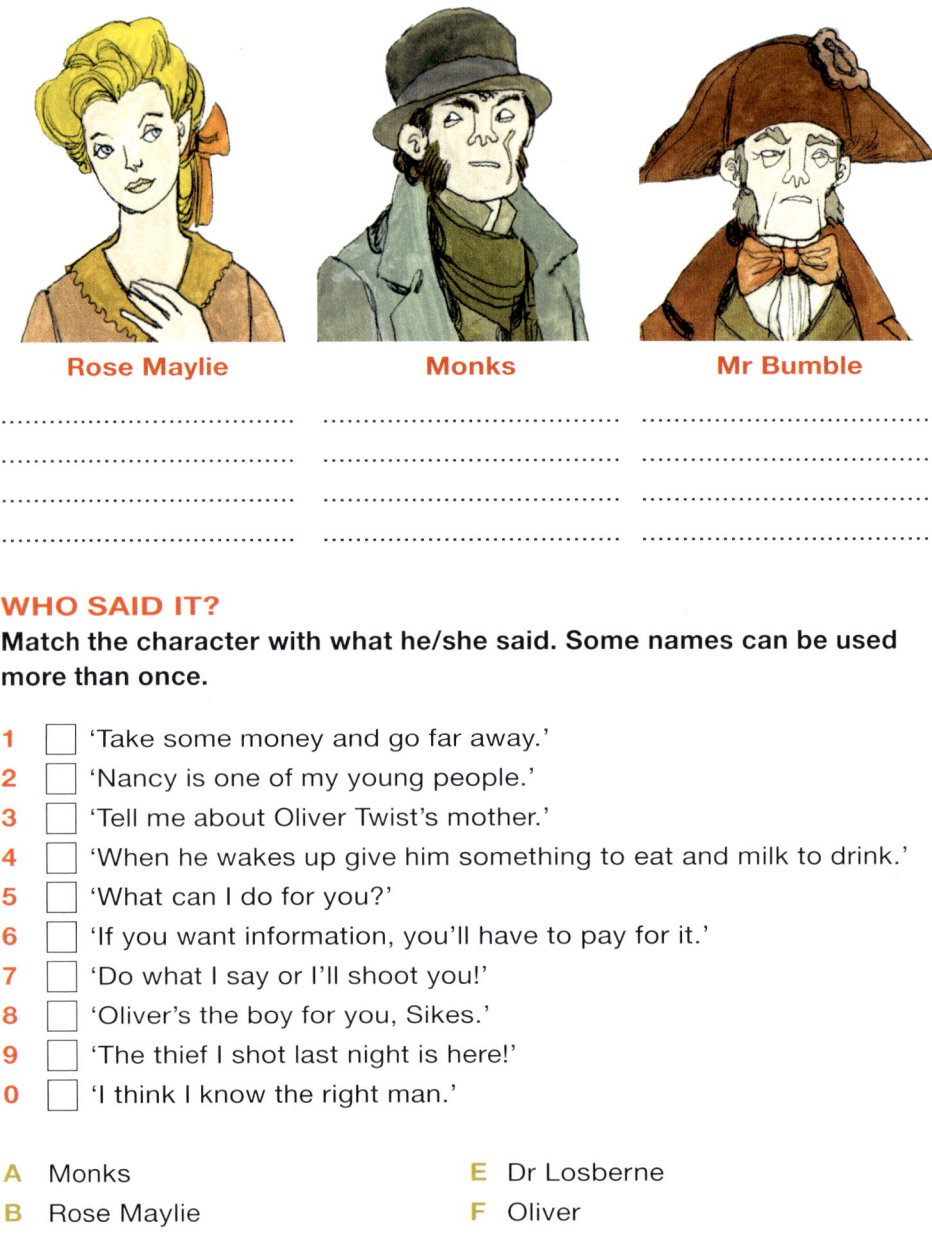

**Rose Maylie**  **Monks**  **Mr Bumble**

..................................  ..................................  ..................................
..................................  ..................................  ..................................
..................................  ..................................  ..................................
..................................  ..................................  ..................................

## 3 WHO SAID IT?
Match the character with what he/she said. Some names can be used more than once.

1. ☐ 'Take some money and go far away.'
2. ☐ 'Nancy is one of my young people.'
3. ☐ 'Tell me about Oliver Twist's mother.'
4. ☐ 'When he wakes up give him something to eat and milk to drink.'
5. ☐ 'What can I do for you?'
6. ☐ 'If you want information, you'll have to pay for it.'
7. ☐ 'Do what I say or I'll shoot you!'
8. ☐ 'Oliver's the boy for you, Sikes.'
9. ☐ 'The thief I shot last night is here!'
10. ☐ 'I think I know the right man.'

A Monks
B Rose Maylie
C Mr Bumble
D Mr Giles
E Dr Losberne
F Oliver
G Bill Sikes
H Fagin

# BEFORE YOU READ

## 1 LISTENING

**Listen to the first part of Chapter Nine and choose the correct answer — A, B, or C.**

1. Why did Rose want to meet Mr Brownlow?
   - A ☐ Because she wanted to tell him about the thieves in her house.
   - B ☐ Because she wanted to tell him Nancy's secret.
   - C ☐ Because she wanted to ask him for money.

2. How did Oliver and Rose get to Mr Brownlow's house?
   - A ☐ on foot
   - B ☐ by train
   - C ☐ by carriage

3. Why did Mr Brownlow and Rose go to the library?
   - A ☐ Because they didn't want Oliver to hear their conversation.
   - B ☐ Because they didn't want Nancy to hear their conversation.
   - C ☐ Because Rose wanted to see Mr Brownlow's books.

4. At what time did the church bell ring on Sunday night?
   - A ☐ At midnight.
   - B ☐ At eleven o'clock.
   - C ☐ At half past eleven.

5. Who followed Nancy to London Bridge?
   - A ☐ Bill Sikes
   - B ☐ Fagin
   - C ☐ one of Fagin's boys

6. Where did Monks stay in London?
   - A ☐ At the King's Hotel in Lion Street.
   - B ☐ At the Red Lion Hotel in King Street.
   - C ☐ At the Red Bridge Hotel in Lion Street.

7. What does Monks have on his face?
   - A ☐ a black mark
   - B ☐ a red mark
   - C ☐ a blue mark

75

CHAPTER **NINE**

# London Bridge

Oliver often thought about Mr Brownlow and his kindness. He wanted to see him again and explain a lot of things.

'Rose, I'd like to go and visit Mr Brownlow,' said Oliver.

'That's a very good idea, Oliver,' said Rose, happily. 'I want to meet him.' She wanted to meet Mr Brownlow and tell him Nancy's secret because she knew he was a good man.

Early in the afternoon Rose and Oliver took a carriage to Mr Brownlow's house. When they arrived Rose said, 'Oliver, please wait in the carriage for a few minutes.'

A servant opened the door of the Brownlow house and Rose followed him to a big sitting room where she met Mr Brownlow. His kind eyes and warm smile made Rose feel welcome.

'Hello, Mr Brownlow. My name is Rose Maylie and I came here to talk about a young boy you know, Oliver Twist.'

'Oliver Twist!' exclaimed Mr Brownlow. 'Do you know Oliver?'

'Yes, I do,' said Rose happily.

76

# London Bridge

'Oh, please sit down and tell me what you know about the poor boy,' said Mr Brownlow.

Rose sat down and told him about Oliver. 'He is such a good boy, with such a kind heart, and we love him very much. And he loves you and Mrs Bedwin.'

'I'm very happy to know that Oliver is well,' said Mr Brownlow, smiling. 'Very happy! But where is he now?'

'He's in the carriage waiting for me,' said Rose.

'Please call him!' said Mr Brownlow. 'Now I'll call Mrs Bedwin.'

Rose went to call Oliver and when he saw Mr Brownlow and Mrs Bedwin he was extremely happy. He hugged them and told them a lot of things. Rose, Oliver, Mr Brownlow and Mrs Bedwin talked and laughed together.

After a while Rose said, 'Mr Brownlow, I'd like to talk to you alone.'

'Of course, Rose,' said Mr Brownlow. 'Please follow me into the library.'

Rose told Mr Brownlow about Nancy's visit and her terrible secret.

Mr Brownlow was very surprised and said, 'What a strange mystery! These people are very cruel. We must find this man called Monks; he knows a lot of things. We must protect Oliver!'

'Yes,' said Rose, 'and only Nancy can help us.'

'But we must wait until Sunday night,' said Mr Brownlow, who was worried.

At eleven o'clock on Sunday night, Fagin and Sikes heard the church bell ring; Nancy heard it too. It was another cold, foggy night in London.

'This is a good night for working,' said Sikes.

'I'm going out, said Nancy. She put on her old coat and left.

Fagin looked at Sikes and said, 'Let her go. One of my boys can follow her!'

# Oliver Twist

Nancy went to London Bridge and met Rose and Mr Brownlow. They went down the steps to the river. One of Fagin's boys followed Nancy to the bridge and hid behind the steps. He listened to everything.

Mr Brownlow said to Nancy. 'Rose and I are here to help Oliver. We want to know about Oliver's mother and father, but only Monks knows about them. We have to find him and learn his secret. Where can we find him?'

Nancy listened to Mr Brownlow and said, 'Yes, Monks knows a lot of things. You can find him at the Red Lion hotel in King Street.'

'What does he look like?' asked Rose.

'He's a man of about twenty-eight,' said Nancy. 'He has black hair and a cruel face. He's tall and always wears a black coat. And he also has a red mark on his neck.'

'A red mark on his neck!' exclaimed Mr Brownlow.

Nancy was surprised and asked, 'Do you know Monks?'

'Perhaps I do,' said Mr Brownlow. 'Can you tell us about Fagin and Sikes? Where can we find them?'

Nancy thought for a moment and said, 'I'm sorry, I can't tell you.' Everyone was silent.

Then Mr Brownlow said, 'I understand, Nancy. Thank you for your help. Now what can we do for you? Please take this money.'

'Yes,' said Rose, 'please take it. We want to help you.'

'You're both very kind,' said Nancy with tears in her eyes, 'but you can't help me. No one can help me. I must go now. God bless you! Good night!' Nancy looked around and then ran up the stairs and disappeared into the foggy night.

Rose and Mr Brownlow were very sorry for Nancy.

'The poor girl has such a difficult life,' said Mr Brownlow sadly.

'Yes, and she has such a kind heart,' said Rose.

Rose and Mr Brownlow went back home in their carriage.

# UNDERSTANDING THE TEXT

## 1 COMPREHENSION CHECK

Read the text below and choose the correct answer — A, B, C or D. The first is done for you.

Oliver often (0) ....D..... about Mr Brown and Mrs Bedwin and their kindness. He told Rose that he wanted to go and see (1) .......... Rose agreed happily (2) .......... she needed to tell Mr Brownlow Nancy's secret.

When Rose and Oliver (3) .......... to Mr Brownlow's house, Oliver remained in the carriage for a (4) .......... minutes while Rose talked to Mr Brownlow. Then Rose called Oliver and he was very happy to see Mr Browlow and Mrs Bedwin. Rose told Mr Brownlow about Nancy's secret and he was (5) .......... and worried.

(6) .......... eleven o'clock on Sunday night Nancy put on her old coat and went to London Bridge, (7) .......... she met Rose and Mr Brownlow. She told them about Monks. One of Fagin's boys followed her and listened to (8) .......... she said.

When Nancy told Mr Brownlow that Monks had a red mark on his neck, Mr Brownlow was surprised because perhaps he knew him. (9) .......... Mr Brownlow asked Nancy about Fagin and Sikes, she didn't say (10) .......... about them. Mr Brownlow offered Nancy some money but she (11) .......... it. She said good-bye, looked (12) .......... and ran up the stairs.

| 0 | A remembered | B believed | C considered | D thought |
|---|---|---|---|---|
| 1 | A they | B him | C them | D their |
| 2 | A because | B so | C why | D how |
| 3 | A reached | B arrived | C got | D getting |
| 4 | A some | B few | C little | D bit |
| 5 | A surprise | B surprising | C surprised | D surprises |
| 6 | A In | B At | C On | D To |
| 7 | A what | B who | C where | D why |
| 8 | A everything | B every | C anything | D any |
| 9 | A Even | B Although | C So | D However |
| 10 | A something | B nothing | C anything | D everything |
| 11 | A refused | B denied | C rejected | D refusal |
| 12 | A at | B over | C for | D around |

## 2 WRITING

**Read the text below and find out about the Victorian Age. Fill in the gaps with the correct past tense of the verbs in the box below. The first is done for you.**

| rule | become (x2) | leave | replace |
| light | grow | create | be | cover |

Queen Victoria (**0**) ...ruled..... longer than any other British monarch: 63 years! During her reign Great Britain (**1**) ............... the richest and most powerful nation in the world. At that time the British Empire (**2**) ............... one-fifth of the earth's land area with about 370 million people. There (**3**) ............... many important changes in the way people lived and worked during the Victorian Age. Many people (**4**) ............... the countryside to work in factories in the big cities. The train (**5**) ............... the carriage and electricity (**6**) ............... streets, homes and public buildings. In other parts of the world photography, telephones and cars (**7**) ............... part of everyday life. Commerce and industry (**8**) ............... rapidly and (**9**) ............... lot of wealth.

**PET**

## 3 LISTENING

**track 14**

**Listen to the story of the two disasters that hit London during the 17th century. Then choose the correct answers — A, B or C.**

1 Which animal carried the plague through London's crowded streets?
 A ☐ a bird  B ☐ a rat  C ☐ a dog

2 When did the Great Fire start?
 A ☐ 2 September  B ☐ 22 September  C ☐ 16 September

3 Where did the Great Fire start?
 A ☐ from a home  B ☐ from a park  C ☐ from a bakery

4 How long did it take Sir Christopher Wren to complete St Paul's Cathedral?
 A ☐ 53 weeks  B ☐ 35 years  C ☐ 35 months

# BEFORE YOU READ

## 1 VOCABULARY

**Match the word with the correct meaning.**

**1** Rope  **2** Devil  **3** Torch  **4** Prison

A ☐

B ☐

C ☐

D ☐

# CHAPTER TEN
# Monks, Sikes and the Others

Late in the night Fagin's boy ran to tell Fagin and Sikes everything he saw and heard at London Bridge.

'What!' cried Fagin. 'Nancy met a man and a woman on London Bridge! I can't believe it! Now we've got big trouble!'

He was furious; his eyes were red and his face was white. He thought about prison and death and he was afraid.

Sikes was also furious [1] and cried, 'I'm going to kill Nancy! I hate her! She has probably told those people all our secrets.' He left Fagin's house and ran to his house. When he got there Nancy was sleeping.

'Wake up, Nancy! Get up!' cried Sikes angrily.

Nancy woke up and saw Sikes near her bed. 'Why are you so angry?' she asked.

---

1. **furious** : very angry.

# Monks, Sikes and the Others

'You went to London Bridge and betrayed[2] us!' said Sikes. 'Now we're in big trouble.'

'Oh, no, Bill! Believe me!' said Nancy, who was very frightened. 'I didn't betray you or Fagin: I didn't say a word. Please believe me!'

'I don't believe you, Nancy!' cried Sikes.

'Listen, Bill. Let's leave this terrible place and go away together,' said Nancy, looking at Sikes. 'We can start a new life together. You know I love you.'

Sikes was furious and didn't listen to Nancy's words. He took his pistol and hit Nancy's face again and again. Poor Nancy fell to the floor. Her face was covered with blood and there was blood everywhere in the room. Nancy was dead!

Sikes's hands were covered with blood and there was blood on his clothes. He washed his hands and face and ran out of the house. His old dog followed him. He decided to go to the country and hide there.

But the people in the country found out about the terrible murder in London and talked about it for many days. Sikes was afraid.

'I can't hide in the country anymore,' he thought. 'The police will find me. I must return to London and hide there for a week. Then I can go to France, where I'll be safe. But first I must kill my dog; everyone knows I have a dog.' Sikes looked for his dog and called it again and again but it ran away.

In London Mr Brownlow, Doctor Losberne and another friend went to the Red Lion hotel and kidnapped Monks. They took him to Rose Maylie's house and locked him in a room.

Monks was very angry and said, 'What are you doing and why? Mr Brownlow, you were my father's good friend!'

'Yes, Monks, I was your father's good friend,' said Mr Brownlow. 'I

2. **betrayed** : gave secret information to someone and this will cause trouble.

# Oliver Twist

know a lot about you and your criminal friends. And I also know you've got a younger brother called Oliver.'

'No!' cried Monks. 'I haven't got a younger brother!'

'You're lying, Monks!' cried Mr Brownlow.

'I'm not lying,' said Monks angrily, 'I haven't got a younger brother.'

'Now listen to me,' said Mr Brownlow seriously. 'I know all about your family history. You're Oliver's half brother because you have the same father but not the same mother. Your mother left your father. He suffered a lot, but then he met and fell in love with a beautiful girl called Agnes. Your father was a rich man. One day he went to Rome for work. Before he left for Rome he told me about Agnes. He made a new will[3] in favour of Agnes and her child, Oliver. In Rome your father became very ill and died.

Your mother knew he was in Rome so she went there. She found the will and did a terrible thing: she burnt it. A few days ago you spoke to Mr and Mrs Bumble. You gave Mrs Bumble some money and she gave you Agnes's ring, which you threw into the river.'

Monks was silent and his face was white. He was very nervous and didn't know what to say.

'I know a lot of other things too,' continued Mr Brownlow. 'I know that poor Nancy is dead; she was murdered! The police want to talk to you, Monks.'

'But I didn't kill Nancy!' cried Monks.

'Hmm, tell that to the police,' said Mr Brownlow. 'They won't believe you.'

'The police…,' said Monks in a low voice, looking at Mr Brownlow.

'Yes, the police,' said Mr Brownlow. 'Or you can sign your name on this piece of paper. It tells the truth about Oliver and his father's

3. **will**: an official document that says who you want to give your money and property to after you die.

## Monks, Sikes and the Others

will. It gives Oliver's money back to him, and you are free to go.'

'But I didn't kill Nancy and I don't work for Fagin!' said Monks. 'Please don't tell the police about me. Just let me go!'

'As soon as you sign this paper, Monks, you can go,' said Mr Brownlow.

Monks was silent for a while and looked at the paper. He was afraid of the police and he didn't want to go to prison.

'Alright, give me that paper,' said Monks nervously. 'I'll sign it!'

He read the paper carefully and signed it.

'Very well, Monks,' said Brownlow, who was satisfied. 'Now you can go.'

Monks got up and quickly left the room and the house.

All of London was talking about Nancy's terrible murder. People everywhere were shocked. The police were looking for Bill Sikes and other criminals. They found Fagin and put him in prison, but Charley Bates and Toby Crackit escaped. They went to stay in an old house on Jacob's Island, which was in the River Thames. It was a poor part of London with a lot of old buildings. The boys were afraid of the police; they didn't want to go to prison.

'We're in danger, Charley,' said Toby Crackit. 'Big danger! Fagin is already in prison and now they're looking for Sikes.'

'Don't worry,' said Charley Bates, 'no one can find us here on Jacob's Island. We're safe.'

There was a loud knock at the door. It was Sikes!

Charley Bates was very angry with Sikes and cried, 'You devil! Why did you kill Nancy? Why?'

Sikes got angry and pushed him to the floor and kicked him. Toby Crackit wanted to fight, but he was afraid of Sikes because he was a strong man.

# Oliver Twist

Suddenly they heard voices outside, 'Murderer! Where's the murderer? Come out in the open! We want to see you!'

Sikes went to the window and saw a lot of angry people with torches in front of the old house.

When the people saw his face at the window they cried, 'There he is! He's the murderer! Let's catch him! Let's break the door!'

Sikes thought about prison and death; he had to escape.

'Listen, Toby, get a long rope,' said Sikes. 'I must escape from the roof on the river side.'

Toby gave Sikes a long rope. He opened a window and went onto the roof with the rope in his hands. It was very dark and his foot slipped. Sikes screamed and fell to the street with the rope around his neck; he was dead!

Fagin was hanged for all his crimes and Charley Bates began a new and honest life. He went to work in the country. Monks went to America but he didn't do any honest work there. He became a thief and died in prison. Mr and Mrs Bumble became very poor and went to live in a workhouse.

Mr Brownlow liked Oliver very much and he adopted [4] him. Oliver grew up and Mr Brownlow sent him to the best schools. After all his adventures Oliver, the orphan, finally found a loving family, true friends and a comfortable home.

---

4. **adopted** : took him into his family and made him legally his son.

# UNDERSTANDING THE TEXT

## 1 COMPREHENSION CHECK
Read the sentences below and choose the correct answer — A, B, C or D.

1 Why were Fagin and Bill Sikes furious?
   - A ☐ Because Nancy ran away.
   - B ☐ Because Nancy talked to the police.
   - C ☐ Because Nancy met some people on London Bridge.
   - D ☐ Because Nancy went to London Bridge with Oliver.

2 Where did Bill Sikes go after he murdered Nancy?
   - A ☐ He went to Fagin's house.
   - B ☐ He went to London Bridge.
   - C ☐ He went to France.
   - D ☐ He went to the country.

3 Who had the same father but a different mother?
   - A ☐ Monks and Oliver
   - B ☐ Agnes
   - C ☐ Bill Sikes and Oliver
   - D ☐ Nancy and Oliver

4 What did Monks's mother do?
   - A ☐ She killed Agnes.
   - B ☐ She destroyed a will.
   - C ☐ She killed her husband in Rome.
   - D ☐ She threw Agnes's ring into the river.

5 Monks signed a piece of paper that
   - A ☐ gave Oliver's money back to him.
   - B ☐ said he killed Nancy.
   - C ☐ gave Oliver's money back to Agnes.
   - D ☐ gave Oliver's money to Mr and Mrs Bumble.

6 What happened to Fagin?
   - A ☐ He went to America.
   - B ☐ He died in prison.
   - C ☐ He was hanged for his crimes.
   - D ☐ He escaped from prison.

7 Who knocked at the door where Charley Bates and Toby Crackit were hiding?
   - A ☐ the police
   - B ☐ some angry people
   - C ☐ Monks
   - D ☐ Bill Sikes

**8** What happened to Bill Sikes?
- A ☐ He fell off the roof and died.
- B ☐ He went to prison and was hanged.
- C ☐ He escaped from the roof.
- D ☐ He went to live in a workhouse.

**PET**

### 2 SENTENCE TRANSFORMATION

For each sentence complete the second sentence so that it means the same as the first. Use no more than three words.

1 'It was such a long book and that's why I didn't like it,' said Oliver.
'I didn't like the book ……………………… so long,' said Oliver.

2 Bill Sikes continued walking in spite of heavy rain.
Although it ……………………… Bill Sikes continued walking.

3 You mustn't talk at the library.
Talking ……………………… at the library.

4 Charles Dickens wrote the famous novel Oliver Twist.
The famous novel Oliver Twist ……………………… Charles Dickens.

5 'If you don't read this book, you won't learn the lesson,' said Mr Brownlow.
'You won't learn the lesson unless you ……………………… said Mr Brownlow.

### FAGIN WAS FURIOUS; HIS EYES WERE RED AND HIS FACE WAS WHITE.

An adjective is a word that describes, identifies, or quantifies nouns and noun phrases. It has only one form and it goes before the noun.

### 3 ADJECTIVES

Adjectives are often used to describe good and bad feelings. Look at the adjectives below and write them in the correct column of the table.

frightened    angry    disappointed    excited    happy
interested    nervous    sad    satisfied    surprised

| GOOD FEELINGS | BAD FEELINGS |
| --- | --- |
|  |  |
|  |  |
|  |  |
|  |  |
|  |  |

Young boys working at midnight in a factory.

# Child Labour

The Industrial Revolution which took place in Great Britain between the late 1700s and the 1800s changed the way people worked and lived. Thousands of families left the country to go and work in factories in the cities. Many of these workers were children and child labour became a big social problem.

Poor families sent their children to work because they needed the money. These children worked long hours in terrible conditions and their jobs were usually dangerous. The factory owners paid them very little money. The children had small fingers and were better at operating some of the machines than adults. They often had to go under the machines to clean them. There were serious accidents and some children died. These children could not go to school, so when they became adults they continued to work in hard jobs for very little money.

The children who didn't work in factories sold flowers and newspapers on the street, or cleaned people's shoes, the streets, or chimneys.[1]

1. **chimney** :

Orphans, like Oliver Twist, and other poor boys often became young thieves, with the help of older criminals like Fagin and Bill Sikes. These young boys didn't have a home or a family and their life was very difficult. Most of them slept in the streets. In 1870 Dr Thomas Barnardo opened the first home for poor boys in London, and gave them food and a warm place to stay.

Some poor children went to a 'Dame' school where a kind woman taught the children reading, writing and simple arithmetic in her own home. Churches and charities sometimes organized 'ragged'[2] schools for very poor children and orphans. There were often as many as one hundred pupils in one classroom, and the older pupils often taught the younger ones.

A young girl works in a cotton mill.

In 1870 the British government passed the Education Act, which said that all children between the ages of five and ten must attend school. However, education was not free and poor families could not send their children to school. Fortunately, after 1891 school became free for all children.

**1 COMPREHENSION CHECK**

Are these sentences true (T) or false (F)? Correct the false ones.

                                                        T  F

1. During the Industrial Revolution the British people became rich.
2. Children who worked did not earn much money.
3. All poor children worked in factories.
4. Dr Thomas Barnardo opened a big hotel in London.
5. Some poor children learned to read and write at a 'Dame' school.
6. Children did not have to pay to go to school after 1891.

  2. **ragged** : the name comes from ragged clothes which were old and torn.

# Filmography

There are over 20 different musical, film and television versions of Dickens's famous novel *Oliver Twist*.
One of the best film versions is, without doubt, *Oliver Twist* directed by Roman Polanski in 2005.
Ben Kingsley plays the part of Fagin and Barney Clark is Oliver.

**Look at the still A and answer the questions.**

1. What's happening and where?
2. How are the characters feeling?
3. What page of the story could this still refer to?

**Look at the still B and answer the questions.**

1. Why is Oliver running away?
2. Who is the gentleman running after Oliver?
3. What has just happened?
4. What will happen next?

# CINEMA

Look at the still C and answer the questions.

1. Who are the characters?
2. Where are they?
3. What is Fagin saying to the boys?
4. Is Fagin similar to the description in the story? Why or why not?

Look at the still D and answer the questions.

1. Who are the characters?
2. What is happening?
3. What is Bill Sikes saying to Oliver?
4. How does Oliver feel?
5. What is going to happen next?

Look at the still E and answer the questions.

1. Describe the scene in detail.
2. Write a caption of your own for this still.

## AFTER READING

**1** Read the sentences below and decide if they are correct or incorrect. If it is correct mark A. If it is not correct mark B.

A　B

1. Oliver Twist and his mother lived in a workhouse for many years.
2. The people at the workhouse were always hungry and cold.
3. Mrs Sowerberry gave Oliver the dog's food to eat but he refused it.
4. Noah Claypole became Oliver's best friend at Mr Sowerberry's shop.
5. Oliver met Jack Dawkins on his way to London.
6. Fagin's jewels and watches belonged to Bill Sikes.
7. One day Oliver stole a gentleman's handkerchief and the police caught him.
8. Mr Brownlow sent Oliver to the bookshop with some books and some money.
9. Oliver was kidnapped by Nancy and Fagin in a small, dark street.
10. Oliver was shot after he entered the Maylie house through the window.
11. Rose Maylie and her aunt adopted Oliver and took him to the countryside.
12. Fagin and Monks went to look for Oliver at the Maylie house.
13. Monks paid Mrs Bumble for Agnes's gold wedding ring.
14. Nancy met Rose Maylie and Mr Brownlow at London Bridge and asked them for money.
15. Bill Sikes and Fagin were furious with Nancy and decided to kill her.
16. Monks signed a paper which told the truth about Oliver and his father's will.
17. The angry crowd of people on Jacob's Island killed Bill Sikes.
18. Mr and Mrs Bumble died in prison and Charley Bates went to America.

**2** Match the description with the character.

1. ☐ He had a box full of beautiful jewels and watches.
2. ☐ She was a lovely young girl who lived with her aunt.
3. ☐ His mother died at a workhouse when he was born.
4. ☐ She was the kind housekeeper at Mr Brownlow's house.
5. ☐ He threw Agnes's gold wedding ring into the river.
6. ☐ He said bad things about Oliver's mother.
7. ☐ He became the master of the workhouse.
8. ☐ She told Rose Maylie about a terrible plan to hurt Oliver.
9. ☐ He took a long rope and wanted to escape from the roof.
10. ☐ He adopted Oliver and sent him to the best schools.
11. ☐ He made coffins for dead bodies.
12. ☐ His real name was Jack Dawkins.
13. ☐ He looked after Oliver's arm when he was hurt.

95

This reader uses the **EXPANSIVE READING** approach, where the text becomes a springboard to improve language skills and to explore historical background, cultural connections and other topics suggested by the text.

The new structures introduced in this step of our **GREEN APPLE** series are listed below. Naturally, structures from lower steps are included too. For a complete list of structures used over all the three steps, see *The Black Cat Guide to Graded Readers*, which is also downloadable at no cost from our website, blackcat-cideb.com.

The vocabulary used at each step is carefully checked against vocabulary lists used for internationally recognised examinations.

## Step 2

All the structures used in the previous steps, plus the following:

**Verb tenses**
Present Perfect Simple: indefinite past with *ever, never* (for experience); indefinite past with *yet, already, still*; recent past with *just*; past action leading to present situation; unfinished past with *for* or *since* (duration form)

**Verb forms and patterns**
*So / neither / nor* + auxiliaries in short answers
Question tags (in verb tenses used so far)
Gerunds (verb + *-ing*) as subjects
Verb + object + full infinitive (e.g. *I want you to help*)

**Modal verbs**
*Should* (present and future reference): advice
*Might* (present and future reference): possibility; permission
*Don't have to / haven't got to*: lack of obligation
*Don't need to / needn't*: lack of necessity

**Types of clause**
Defining relative clauses with: *which, that*, zero pronoun
Time clauses introduced by *when, while, until, before, after, as soon as*
Clauses of purpose: *(in order) to* (infinitive of purpose)

**Other**
Comparative and superlative of adverbs (regular and irregular)